Award-Winning
Portugal Living
Magazine

Portugal in the Movies

João Gonzalez, Director
Ice Merchants

Running a B&B
Assisted Living
Your Last Rites
Selling Portugal
Let's Talk Money
Top Expat Attorneys
A Master Bladesmith
Jamming in Portugal
Reverence for Books
Minding Your Manners
Known by Their Names
7 Weeks in the Alentejo
The Thing about Visitors
Cork—Aboard & Abroad
15 'Cheap' Cities with Quality
The Myth of Becoming a Local
Return of Roman Winemaking
What I've Learned to Accept
Scoundrels Distillery and Gin School
Conimbriga: Coimbra's Roman Ruins
Renovating an 1812 Lisbon Apartment
Becoming A Better Person In Portugal
11 Reasons You Shouldn't Move to Portugal
A Walk in the Steps of Portugal's Knights Templar

Plus:
• News & Information
• Friends & Neighbors
• Concerts & Performances
• Up Your Portuguese!
• Caption Contest & Photo Finish

viv|europe

You can count on Viv Europe

to **facilitate** your **relocation** to Portugal.

We can help you:

- Compile and prepare documents needed to apply for a Portuguese Visa
- Create your Portuguese Tax Number (NIF) and open a bank account for you
- Search and select properties in Portugal, whether for lease or purchase
- Secure Certificates and all Visa-related documents

Contact us with your questions at
contact@viveurope.com

Meet our team

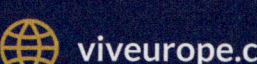 viveurope.com

 +351 934 103 844

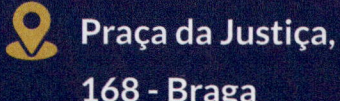 Praça da Justiça, 168 - Braga

FOLLOW US:

TJ PROPERTY INSPECTIONS

Purchasing property in Portugal? Before you buy, have us inspect it!

We offer expert pre-purchase inspections for buyers and vendors in Portugal, the Azores, Spain, Italy, and beyond.

- ✓ 35 years' experience
- ✓ The latest equipment and techniques
- ✓ A personal, professional service

Get in touch with us now!

✉ info@tjpropertyinspections.com

📞 +351 915 985 243

tjpropertyinspections.com

Bem Vindos!

In Search of Publisher-Creative Director for award-winning magazine serving English language "expats" and "wannabes" in Portugal.

For sale, acquisition, partnership, or pick-up-the-pieces.

Although I am passionate about producing this thoughtful magazine for people with Portugal on their minds, I'm burned out … turning 75 … with other stories to tell, songs to sing, windmills to challenge, places to explore, and voids to plug.

Publisher-Creative Director responsibilities include:

- Represent magazine through correspondence, interviews, webinars, guest appearances;
- Maintain and increase subscription and advertiser base;
- Recruit, engage, negotiate, and invoice advertisers;
- Develop balanced content of interest to those planning to relocate to Portugal, recent newcomers, and residents;
- Assign and oversee writer, photographer, and artist submissions;
- Write articles and other elements of the magazine;
- Oversee graphic design to maintain brand integrity;
- Edit, proofread, and approve all content per style guide;
- Lay out magazine to ensure equitable and attractive balance of columns, departments, features, and advertising;
- Secure illustrations or artwork to complement the articles;
- Create print editions of magazine for sale on Amazon;
- Update daily Facebook "mini-magazine";
- Connect and post daily on social media network accounts: Facebook, Instagram, YouTube, LinkedIn;
- Coordinate and create components of magazine's website;
- Interface with database (Mailchimp), mailing company (Send in Blue), and IT coordinator to distribute digital subscriptions;
- Promote and publicize the magazine and its contents.

I've yet to take a cent from the magazine … more often than not, digging deeper into my own pockets for funds. And, yeah, it's a lot of work—but the payoff is priceless!

All offers considered to keep our *magnus opus* going and growing.

Interested? Please contact me at: portugallivingmagazine@gmail.com.

What if we can't find someone(s) with the expertise, sensitivity, and resources to invest in this venture?

We'll just have to adapt and adjust.

Bruce H Joffe
Publisher & Creative Director

Portugal Living Magazine
Issue No. 9—Summer 2023

Contributors
Walt Bosmans
Margaux Cintrano
Deborah Dahab
Sarah Davie
Brian Elliott
Kristin Fellows
James F. Hickey
Justin Knepper
Yvonne Landry
Diana Laskaris
Alistair Leithead
Susan Lindsey
Fernando Mendes
Lea Melo
Carl Munson
Jayme Henriques Simões
Beth Thomas-Kim
Rob Vajko
Carol A. Wilcox
LaDonna Witmer

Website Coordinator
Sarah Sibert

Design Director
Russ Warren

Publisher/Creative Director
Bruce H. Joffe

Portugal Living Magazine. Volume Three, Issue Nine. Copyright ©2023 by *Portugal Living Magazine*. All rights reserved. Opinions expressed on these pages are those of the authors and do not necessarily represent the magazine. *Portugal Living Magazine* is published quarterly: Summer, Fall, Winter, and Spring. Website: http://www.portugallivingmagazine.com. Email: portugallivingmagazine@gmail.com.

cover photo: Unifrance

ExpatsPortugal is the leading organisation in Portugal assisting people to move here and those that have already arrived.
We have a friendly and vibrant community with circa. 12,000 members and growing. Meet online and in person, ask your questions, share experiences and learn about life in Portugal. Not just from expats but also from our many Portuguese members.

We can also guide you through all the requirements to move here through our carefully selected and approved professional partners covering visa, fiscal, legal, healthcare, money transfer, insurance, mortgages, removals, property search, taxation, motor vehicles and lots more.
WWW.EXPATSPORTUGAL.COM

CONTENTS

 42
 58
 60
 64
 66

4	Bem Vindos!	66	A Walk in the Steps of Portugal's Knights Templar
8	Feedback	68	Conímbriga: Portugal's Largest Roman Ruins
10	Editorial	71	11 Reasons You Shouldn't Move to Portugal
12	Rant!	75	Assisted Living in Portugal
15	Q&A	78	Lessons Learned from 7 Weeks in the Alentejo
16	Noteworthy	80	Becoming a Better Person in Portugal
32	Let's Talk Money	82	The Return of Roman Winemaking
34	Selling Portugal	85	Last Rites
36	What I've Learned to Accept …	88	People Want to Be Known by Name
38	Minding Your Manners	90	The Myth of Becoming a Local
40	Expat Attorneys in Portugal	92	Up Your Portuguese!
42	A Belgian Restores an 1820 Lisbon Apartment	93	My Story: Amada
44	Portugal's Starring Roles	94	Neighbors
48	15 'Cheap' Cities with a High Quality of Life	96	Espectáculos
52	Cork, Aboard and Abroad	97	Caption Contest
54	A Master Bladesmith	98	Classifieds
56	Reverence for Books	99	Business & Professional Directory
58	Jamming in Portugal	100	*Portugal Living Magazine* to Cease PDF-Format Production
60	From Desk Job to Running a B&B	101	Photo Finish
62	The Thing about Visitors		
64	Scoundrels Distillery and Gin School		

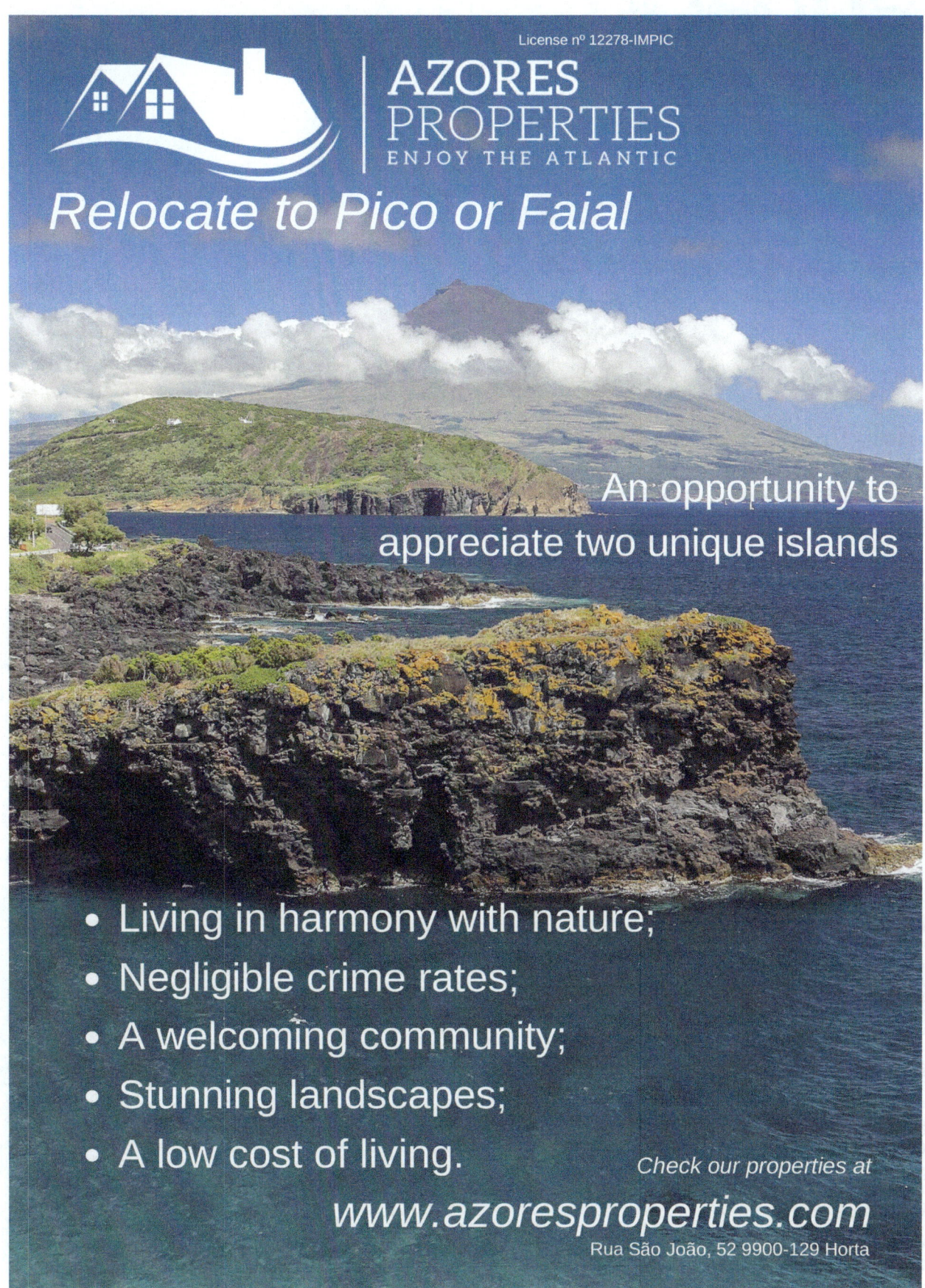

Feedback

About Our Last Issue

The story about importing cars to Portugal contains inaccuracies.

It states that ISV free import is only available to those on NHR. That is incorrect, any new resident can import a car free of ISV if they meet the conditions, having NHR is not one of the conditions.

It also states that ISV isn't payable on cars imported from elsewhere in the EU. This is also incorrect; it doesn't matter where the car is imported from, ISV is due on all cars imported to Portugal (it's a first registration fee).

The story claims that Portuguese citizens can claim ISV exemption if they've lived outside Portugal for more than six months. Actually. it's 24 months.

Similarly, any IVA (VAT) or ISV due does not have to be paid within 20 days of importing the car.

Due to these inaccuracies, this story only adds to the false information that abounds regarding importing cars to Portugal. The story would have been more beneficial to readers had the author fact-checked what they had written by reading the *Código do Imposto sobre Veículos*. The relevant EU Directive (2009/55/EC) at Article 1 specifies that the tax-free movement of personal goods does <u>not</u> apply to motor vehicles.
Emmjay Hay

Like you, I have found some regularly posted publications centered on the Algarve area. Which is so very different than the rest of the country. I applaud this endeavor. One quick note—there's a spelling error in the beginning area. A small thing, but I believe in your precision in communication. Simply a space missing between two words: "*Portugal Living Magazine* took root and flourishedtook root and …"
Lisa Funston

Thanks, Lisa. No matter how many times or how many different eyes an issue is proofread, there's always at least one that got away. You can proof for us anytime you like!

Since when I did grant you permission to repost articles from my blog to your magazine? I thought you came about your content legitimately, but it's clear that you make a practice of stealing content for your own purposes. This makes *Portugal Living Magazine* nothing more than a content farm, hardly a magazine at all.
Gail Aguiar

Portugal Living Magazine is fortunate to benefit from a number of sources for its content. Most of our features are original. As is this magazine. Several are blog posts which we thought were outstanding and sought permission to share. Most bloggers are delighted to expand their reach through republishing something they wrote with a "Share" button affixed. Still, we make every effort to contact the blogger and ask permission to reprint his or her story. At the article's conclusion, we attribute our source(s), give a bio of the blogger, and hyperlink to his or her blog site.

Suggested topic for future issue: How prepared is Portugal for an environmental disaster? Earthquake? Typhoon? With the entire Atlantic Ocean occupying the Western Boarder I would think the possibility of a future weather-related incident would be high. Not to mention possibility of earthquake similar to what happened in Turkey/Syria. Who oversees building codes in Portugal?
Ronald S Bramson

There is so much interesting and useful information and I know some of the people that are advertising and writing. Congratulations! I´m already looking forward to the next edition.
Anne Brightman

Enjoyed [Deborah Dahab](#)'s article on making friends.
[Jenny Ives](#)

A sensational edition! I noticed higher resolution photography, more elegant lettering fonts, and much better photography selections.

Congratulations on another successful release.
Nandini Singh

Another great issue!
[Diana Laskaris](#)

Great variety of topics! Well done.
Walt Bosmans

Have something to say about this new issue … or *Portugal Living Magazine*? Please share it with us:
letters@portugallivingmagazine.com

Portuguese Fed Up with Incentives for Foreign Home Buyers

(Bloomberg) — Pressure is mounting within Portugal to cut incentives for foreign home buyers as the country grapples with rising property prices and a shortage of affordable housing.

A survey commissioned by weekly newspaper Expresso found that 90% of respondents agree that Portugal is in the midst of a housing crisis. With outside demand continuing to drive up property prices, more than half of those surveyed say they want the government to roll back incentives for foreign buyers.

The poll, which was carried out last month by ICS and ISCTE university institutes and questioned more than 800 people, took place after home prices rose 13% from a year earlier in the third quarter, according to the country's statistics institute. That's the second-biggest increase since the institute started collecting data on the housing market in 2010.

More than three-fourths of those surveyed blame the crisis on a lack of public investment in housing, insufficient regulation and a shortage of available units. Some 64% said that incentives for foreign buyers, such as the so-called "golden visa" program that grants foreign nationals a residency permit in exchange for a real estate investment, were impacting the situation.

Foreigners have flocked to Portugal in recent years in search of a warm climate and lower costs of living. According to an April report from the statistics institute, these buyers are willing to pay more than double for a home in Lisbon than their local counterparts.

To try to regulate demand, Portugal's government in 2021 began restricting its golden visa program to property purchases outside Lisbon and the northern city of Porto. It also plans to increase the share of public housing from 2% to 5% of all housing in coming years.

Henrique Almeida, Bloomberg News

©2023 Bloomberg L.P.

Rant!

I don't enjoy the bacalhau, pastel de nata (room temp custard—really? That's your national dessert item?), grilled sardines, francesinhas, and/or bifanas. There's a reason this food isn't found outside of Portugal much, relative to just about any other cuisine.

Yes, a huge plus is how cheap everything is. But if you don't like, let's say "bifana," what difference does it make?

Dousing a ham and cheese sandwich with tomato-based sauce and throwing an egg on top and naming it something having to do with France is an abomination—even the most basic ham and cheese sandwich or anything between two slices of bread, for that matter, will be tastier and better for your health. Plus, soggy fries because of said sauce? WTH!

If you like boring boiled baby yellow potatoes with every meal, this definitely is the place for you.

Here is an unsolicited opinion from a friend who stayed here three weeks:

"Once you get over the initial shock that every Portuguese restaurant serves large octopus and clam dishes, it becomes apparent that Portuguese food really sucks. It's mostly over salted stuff from cans, salty fish, and boiled vegetables. The entire cuisine seems oriented around being exportable by ship (they are a sea-faring nation after all)."

The other dishes that everyone raves about are just Instagrammable.

Everyone posts these dumb Cafe Santiago Francesinha sandwiches with the egg on top and I could see that the people in the videos were never impressed by the taste; rather, they just thought it was an impressive sight. But that sandwich literally is horrible for you and tastes worse than a ham and cheese or even Russian/French/Spanish salami between bread. A croissant. Anything, really.

Yeah—cool that you figured out something unique, Porto, but c'mon.

I hope to move to Portugal one day. But it won't be for the food. As much as I rag on Portugal food, I have had some amazing food there. But that was a two-hour drive into the mountains in the middle of the country.

The opinions expressed in Rant do not necessarily reflect the opinions of the *Portugal Living Magazine* publisher and directors.

MEDAL INSURANCE

Since 1996

afpop ADvantage
ALLIANCE PARTNER

Portugal's leading Insurance Brokers for Expats

HEALTH

An **Exclusive Health Insurance** specially designed to suit your particular needs. Our scheme represents **the best value for money** you can find in the Portuguese market.

- No age limit
- Exclusive and Unique conditions at the Portuguese Market
- Acceptance of Clinical History from previous insurers
- Any Doctor or Hospital / Clinic in Portugal

HOUSEHOLD

Main Benefits:

Third Party Liability
(Including Rentals)

Jewellery and Valuables
(All Risks – Worldwide)

Many Optional Covers such as:
Electrical Risks and Accidental Damages

MOTOR

Main Benefits:

Fully Comprehensive cover
available for vehicles up to 10 years

No Excess

Any Driver

Exclusive Rates

TRAVEL

Main Benefits:

Cover for Death, Sudden illness
or Accident

No age Limit

Worldwide cover

Trip cancellation and Curtailment

As your Insurance Broker, we are able to provide exclusive products and a professional advice for all your insurance needs through our dedicated team and give you personalised service throughout all your claims processes.

Ask us for a quote to benefit from our unique products for **AFPOP members**

PORTIMÃO HEAD OFFICE:
R. Dr. Teófilo Braga, 3A - 1º
8501-919 Portimão
Tel.: +351 282 430 800

ALMANCIL OFFICE:
Av. José dos Santos Farias, Lt. 83, R/C Dto.
8135-167 Almancil
Tel.: +351 289 351 000

ESTORIL OFFICE:
Av. Sabóia, 487 C/D
2765-298 Monte do Estoril
Tel.: +351 210 523 130

www.medal.pt
info@medal.pt

MEDAL – Gestão e Mediação de Seguros, Lda. Mediador de seguros inscrito, em 27/01/2007, no registo da ASF-Autoridade de Supervisão de Seguros e Fundos de Pensões com a categoria de Agente de Seguros, sob o Nº 407154810/3, com autorização para os ramos VIDA e NÃO VIDA verificável em www.asf.com.pt - Membro APROSE com o n.º 634, verificável em www.aprose.pt

13 Portugal Living Magazine

askfernando.pt

Insurance
Home Internet
Mobile Phone Plans
Mortgages
Funeral Direction

"Fernando is professional, quick and efficient, and English-speaking. All my insurance renewals have saved me money ... My car insurance was 100 euros cheaper this year."
— Susan Cox

"An absolute legend, this is how we describe Fernando. From sorting out our bank account to getting us connected to the internet, all within a week."
— Nicole Barnes

Trust Fernando for the best service and prices in the market.

Get the help you need now!
askfernando.pt

Can someone, please, explain why every airbnb (apartment, condo, or house) I have stayed in here in Portugal cannot have more than a couple appliances going without flipping the circuit breaker? Why aren't the circuits able to handle the load of multiple appliances? If I were to own property, would it be possible to remedy this problem in my own house or condo/apartment?

In these cases, the contracted power is less than the consumption of the equipment that is connected at that time. The contracted power makes it possible, therefore, to know the amount of equipment that can be connected simultaneously, so the more equipment you want to connect, the greater the contracted power must be.

Electricity customers can contract 13 different powers from electricity suppliers.

In the residential sector, the most common contracted power values are between 3.45 and 6.9 KVA.

When choosing the contracted power, you should consider the energy class of your equipment (the better the energy class, the lower the consumption) and the number of appliances that must be connected simultaneously to carry out your daily tasks.

If you find that the contracted power is above or below your daily needs, you can request a change in the contracted power from your electric company.

Source: PoupaenergiaPT

Welcome to the Best Selection of Groceries in Europe!

€18.99 Flat Rate Shipping through Mondial Relay to Portugal!

@americangroceriesbelgium

Noteworthy

More than 90,000 ask parliament to criminalize animal abuse

A petition from União Zoófila with more than 90,000 signatures defending the criminalization of mistreatment of animals was delivered at the Assembly of the Republic. To be discussed in parliament, a petition needs a minimum of 7,500 signatures, which is why the organizing committee of the petition refers to being "certain" that this "will be discussed very soon" in the Assembly of the Republic, "raising the presentation of projects legislation on these matters."

The petition gathered 12,000 signatures in just 36 hours and more than 90,000 in just one month, according to the statement.

"The petitioners appeal to the Constitutional Court to promote an ethical and up-to-date interpretation of our fundamental law, including the protection of animals, and to the Assembly of the Republic to extend criminal protection to sentient animals, not just companion animals, which improve the rules in force and include the express reference to animals in the text of the Constitution."
Source: Safe Communities Portugal

Number of new companies in Portugal up 21.2%

In 2021, Portugal had more than 1.3 million companies, of which 187,036 were started in that year, an increase of 21.2% compared to 2020. These figures, according to data published by the National Institute of Statistics (INE), show an approximation to the levels of the constitution of companies in 2019, the last year before the Covid-19 pandemic, when the number of new companies was 196,193 — that is, just 4.7% more compared to 2021.

According to the report "Companies in Portugal — Demografia das Empresas" and reported by ECO, the proportion of companies still active one year after starting stood at 75.7%, 1.1 percentage points (p.p.) higher than in 2020 and minus 0.4 p.p. compared to 2019, while those that survived three years after opening corresponded to 49.1% (4.9 p.p. more compared to 2020 and 2.9 p.p. more compared to 2019).
Source: The Portugal News

Car of the Year in Portugal

The Car of the Year/Volante de Cristal Trophy Award 2023 has been awarded to the Renault Austral, which succeeds the Peugeot 308.

According to NM, this is the first time in 20 years that the French manufacturer has been distinguished with the award, with the last time being in 2003 with the Renault Mégane.

Among 22 candidates on the list, the final was decided between seven cars, with the Austral receiving the highest number of votes from the national jury.

Renault's SUV won over the Honda Civic, Nissan Ariya, Peugeot 408, Renault Mégane E-TECH Electric, Skoda Fabia and the Volkswagen ID. Buzz.
Source: The Portugal News

Lisbon wants to fix housing shortage by becoming a major landlord

Lisbon mayor Carlos Moedas announced that funds from the Recovery and Resilience Plan (PRR) available for the post-Covid economic boost would be used to purchase more residential buildings from private owners. The aim of the plan is to increase the supply of affordable rental housing in a city that desperately needs more of that.

The idea to make City Hall one of the major players in the rental market originated from Housing Councilor Filipa Roseta. The plan was launched immediately to mitigate the housing crisis conditions plaguing the Portuguese capital.

The focus of the local administration would thus be not to boost and compete in the construction development sector but rather to buy properties that have already been built and renovate them if necessary. There are many abandoned or decaying buildings that need a "facelift"

before being put back on the housing rental market at subsidized prices for those in need of a place to call home.
Source: The Mayor.eu

Portugal maintains BBB+ rating

The financial rating agency Standard and Poor's (S&P) reaffirmed the assessment of Portuguese sovereign debt at 'BBB+', with a stable outlook.

In a report, S&P explains that the stable outlook reflects the expectation "that the high levels of public and external debt in Portugal will continue to decline, balancing the risks to economic growth and the budgetary trajectory arising from a potential stagflation in the Europe" and the uncertainty of the geopolitical context.

The agency points out that it expects that Portugal will present primary budget surpluses in the coming years, which will allow it to reduce the net debt in relation to the Gross Domestic Product (GDP) below 100%, even though the cost of issuing debt should increase.
Source: TPN/Lusa

Portugal: top destination for foreign retirees

International Living's 2023 Annual Global Retirement Index confirmed Portugal as the top destination for retirees, with Mexico and Panama securing second and third place on the podium, respectively.

The study evaluated 16 countries based on factors such as climate, cost of living, safety, culture, lifestyle, and healthcare services. Ecuador, Costa Rica, Spain, Greece, and France complete the top eight of the list.

With recent data from Brussels, cited by business newspaper *Jornal de Negócios,* reveals that Portugal has the highest proportion of pensions paid by foreign social security systems among the 32 European countries with common social protection mobility rules.
Source: The Portugal News

Portuguese post office launches crypto stamp and NFT
The Portuguese post office (CTT) launched the first Portuguese crypto stamp, issued in physical format and in NFT ('Non-Fungible Token'), "with exclusive benefits for collectors," launched under the theme "Navigating to discover the future."

The launch of the first Portuguese crypto stamp "reinforces CTT's role as one of the most disruptive and active postal operators in the development of new products and services in all areas of the company, including philately," says the company led by João Bento, and reported by JN.

The development of the crypto stamp was done in partnership with the Estonian startup Stampsdaq, a company dedicated to cooperation with postal operators around the world, bridging the gap with collectors, say CTT.
Source: The Portugal News

What worries Portuguese people?

A study by IKEA concludes that at the top of the concerns of life at home for the Portuguese is the national economy (85%), followed by climate change and domestic finances.

According to the findings, one in every 10 people who participated in the study anticipates that the increase in the cost of living will affect important moments, such as getting married and having children, and almost half (49%) anticipate that their hobbies and interests away from home are negatively impacted.

"The Portuguese show more concern about climate change (78%) than the global average of 37 countries participating in the study (56%)," the information states, according to NM.

The study also indicates that "67% of respondents in Portugal feel that their home reflects who they are, a figure that drops to 56% among young people" and that "the three main frustrations at home are related to clutter (34%), housework (30%), and not having outside space (27%)".
Source: The Portugal News

Rush for golden visas after Portugal ends criticised scheme

Portugal's plan to end its golden visa scheme for investors has led to a rush in applications, according to advisory firms who have criticised the plan.

Aimed at non-EU nationals ready to invest in Portugal, the visa attracted 6.8 billion euros ($7.30 billion) since its launch in 2012, with the bulk of the money going to real estate. Successful applicants receive residency rights.

The golden visa has been heavily criticised at home for sending house prices up, and the European Commission has called for the end of such programs. As part of a package to address the housing crisis as rents also soar, Portugal's premier Antonio Costa announced his intention to scrap the scheme.

Armand Arton, head of Arton Capital, which helps people get a second residency or citizenship via investment, said his firm had seen a 50% jump in applications since the announcement.
Source: FXEmpire

Portugal tops Spain for Americans seeking to move abroad

Analysis of Google data by My Dolce Casa has found that Portugal was 2022's most searched for European country by Americans interested in moving abroad.

According to the site: "More and more Americans are considering moving abroad in search of a better quality of life, safety and good weather, and Europe has long been a favourite destination that checks these boxes. But one European country has been much talked about throughout 2022 as a highly sought-after destination to live in: Portugal."

During 2022, searches for Portugal each month topped 41,200, demonstrating a year-on-year increase of 30 percent, and knocking long-time favourite Spain off the most desired country to live in.

My Dolce Casa continues: "In 2022, Spain was Americans' second favourite country to live in, with 38,900 average monthly Google searches, up 9% from 2021. At a great distance behind was Germany, with 15,300 searches, followed by Ireland with 13,200 and Italy, surprisingly only in fifth place, with a combined 12,600 searches per month.

"Moreover, Portugal saw the highest percentage and net increase in Google searches compared to the previous year, when Spain was the definitive leader, with 35,400 monthly searches in 2021. Simpler, less stringent immigration requirements and lower taxes have given Portugal an edge over Spain. It is worth noting that Portugal is about five times smaller in size compared to Spain, which makes this tiny but mighty country's achievement even more impressive.
Source: The Portugal News

Portugal's Tage Studios promises to be Europe's first entirely green shooting facility

With solar panels, a rainwater recovery system, an effort to preserve local biodiversity and an emphasis on using recycled materials, the facility intends to be "eco-friendly and self-sustainable from day one."

Just outside of Lisbon, plans are underway to build Europe's, and maybe the world's, first truly green film studio. The €200 million ($215 million) Tage Studios project, which is set to begin breaking ground near the town of Palmela, southeast of Lisbon, in late 2024 or early 2025, would be the first backlot in Europe built top to bottom with environmental sustainability in mind. Every soundstage and facility building is designed to be a near-zero-energy structure, with rooftop photovoltaic panels providing electricity and rainwater recovery and reuse systems cutting down on water waste. Landscaping will be done to ensure preservation of local biodiversity. Even much of the material used for construction will be locally sourced and/or recycled, with at least 85 percent recovery of all site construction waste.

"The idea was to create a benchmark studio, one that will be eco-friendly and self-sustainable from day one, making it the world's first for film and television facilities," says David Hallyday, founder and director of Tage Studios (and, in his day job, a French singer-songwriter and son of late Gallic rock legend Johnny Hallyday, aka the "French Elvis"). "When we started this project, five years ago now, we couldn't find any studio anywhere that was designed like this, to be a green facility from the start."
Source: The Hollywood Reporter

Portuguese pastry best in the world

The national cuisine of Portugal has again been recognised with four pastries making the top 100 in the world –and the top two spots also going to Portugal.

In first place in the rankings by Taste Atlas is the Pastel de Bélem, with second place going to the more widely served Pastel de nata.

Also noteworthy is the Bola de Berlim, which placed 26th. The last national sweet mentioned in this list appears in 94th position: Travesserios from Sintra.

The Italian focaccia di recco, the Swedish kanelbulle and the Bulgarian banitsa round off the top five on this list, which also includes other suggestions made with puff pastry.
Source: The Portugal News

Direct flights between Lisbon and Boston

Delta Air Lines will resume the summer service of daily direct flights between Lisbon and Boston, from May 9 until October 27.

In total, Delta Air Lines will operate up to 14 weekly flights between Portugal and the U.S. during the summer with a capacity of up to 430 seats per day.
Source: The Portugal News/Lusa

Portugal's renewables, air quality, better than average

Portugal performs well in areas such as renewable energy, greenhouse gas emissions and air quality but needs to improve in waste recovery and the circular economy, according to an OECD report.

The Organisation for Economic Cooperation and Development (OECD) published its fourth review of Portugal's environmental performance, providing 26 recommendations to help it "strengthen policy coherence to drive a green economic recovery" and make progress on carbon neutrality and sustainable development.

"Portugal is lagging in relation to the circular economy," the document reads, adding that "urban waste generation grew faster than the economy. In 2020, Portugal generated more urban waste 'per capita' than the European average. It was also one of the countries with the highest landfill rates." And for 2020, the country "did not meet most of its waste targets."

Regarding urban wastewater treatment, Portugal is well above the EU average with 92% compared to 76%, the OECD said. Agricultural water collection, however, has increased by around 25% since the mid-2010s.
Source: Euractiv

Growing tourism while reducing emissions

Portugal and Italy have joined an elite group of countries that have managed to grow their travel and tourism industry, while reducing carbon emissions intensity.

The achievement was revealed as part of an ongoing series of data being released by the World Travel & Tourism Council (WTTC) and the Saudi-based Sustainable Tourism Global Center. The research effort is one of the largest of its kind and is focused on accurately reporting and tracking the impact the travel and tourism sector has on the environment.
Source: Travel Pulse

GP DESIGN
GONÇALO PYRRAIT
DECORATION • FABRICS & MATERIALS • PROJECTS

"ATELIER" • RUA JOÃO PENHA, 10
1250-131 LISBOA PORTUGAL
+351 966 472 292 • GONCALOPYRRAIT@GMAIL.COM
WWW.GP-DESIGN.EU

Iberia increases Portugal summer offer by 18%
This summer, Iberia will make 730,000 seats available on routes to Portugal, an offer that represents an 18% growth compared to the pre-pandemic period and which maintains operations to Faro and Ponta Delgada.

"During the summer season, which starts on March 25th and ends on October 28th, Iberia booked more than 730,000 seats with Portugal, 18% more than in 2019, and, in August, the busiest month, scheduled 79 weekly frequencies, 25% more than in 2019," highlights Iberia in a statement and shared by Publituris.

Iberia's summer offer also brings back the routes from Faro and Ponta Delgada to Madrid, the first of which will run between June and September, while the operation to the capital of São Miguel will take place between July and September.

In the case of Faro, the operation will have three flights a week, moving to a daily flight in August, which will be operated by Iberia Regional/Air Nostrum, in a CRJ1000 aircraft, with capacity for 100 passengers.

In July, Iberia resumes flights to Ponta Delgada, in the Azores, an operation that will also have three flights a week until September, on Mondays, Wednesdays and Saturdays, the route being operated on an A320 aircraft with capacity for 180 passengers.
Source: The Portugal News

Government Scraps VAT on "Essential Items"
In its latest effort to tackle the cost-of-living crisis, the government scrapped VAT on a group of "essential items" between April and October, Público reports. The measure, which follows a similar move in Spain, is expected to cost the state about €410 million and the government says it is being developed under the assumption of a commitment from producers and supermarkets to pass the savings on to customers. The list itself is still unknown but is said to include healthy food, much of which is already taxed at the reduced VAT (IVA) rate of 6%. According to Público, the list features 46 products, including bacalhau but not salmon, and the items won't be available tax-free until the change passes through parliament.
Source: Safe Communities Portugal

Calls for 0% VAT on tofu, too
The PAN political party has proposed to the Government that foods based on vegetable protein, such as tofu and seitan, should also have zero VAT, warning that "about one million" Portuguese opt for a vegetarian diet.
Source: TPN/Lusa

North Americans leading Portugal investment
International funds led real estate transactions in Portugal during 2022, representing more than 85% of the total, with North Americans heading the list.

Attractive property prices in Portugal, combined with the high liquidity of the market, led foreign funds to invest heavily in Portuguese real estate. According to Nuno Nunes, head of capital markets at CBRE, "real estate funds have a dominant market share in the Portuguese market," which represents over 85 percent in recent years, cites *Jornal de Negócios*.

The biggest transaction ever in the Portuguese real estate market, the purchase of the Crow project for 800 million euros, was sealed by the US fund Davidson Kempner.
Source: The Portugal News

photo: Lusa

Rules for electric scooters in Portugal
The Public Security Police (PSP) has highlighted some rules that scooter users must consider when circulating with these vehicles.

"The PSP appeals to all citizens who, daily or casually, use electric scooters, to do so with respect for other users of the public road, whether for their own safety or for the safety of others," reads the Facebook post from the force.

The PSP thus reminds that scooters must circulate on cycle paths or, when these do not exist, on the carriageway. On the sidewalks, only "children up to 10 years old, who do not put pedestrians in danger," can circulate.
Source: TPN

Portugal The Place
A DESTINATION MANAGEMENT COMPANY
www.portugaltheplace.com

We are a full-service destination management company providing relocation and home scouting across the entire country. Our team is here to help you navigate your move to Portugal.

WE ARE YOUR SNEAKERS ON THE GROUND

- Location Scouting
- Long-term Rental Scouting
- Home Scouting
- Relocation Support

SCHEDULE A FREE CONSULTATION CALL ON OUR WEBSITE OR CONTACT US FOR MORE INFORMATION

www.portugaltheplace.com

1+351 961 315 405 | WhatsApp

inquires@portugaltheplace.com

Portugal to increase tourism sector workers by 20%

Portugal's Ministry of the Interior has introduced a new initiative with a total of 20 measures, including the plan to increase the number of workers in the tourism industry by a total of 20 per cent.

"This is a strategic agenda, with 20 measures, which aims to surge by 10 per cent the number of tourism professionals with secondary and higher education, and to increase by 15 per cent the number of students in tourism at all levels of education and to increase by 20 per cent the number of people employed in the sector," the Ministry of the Economy and Maritime Affairs pointed out in this regard.

According to the Nuno Fazenda, the measures also include the national plan for modernisation as well as specialisation of the hotel as well as tourism school network and the implementation of an international tourism academy.
Source: Schengenvisa

New Portuguese Netflix series announced

The Portuguese series *Rabo de Peixe* arrived in May on Netflix.

Produced by Ukbar Filmes, *Rabo de Peixe* is the second Portuguese series for Netflix made entirely in Portugal, after *Glória,* by Tiago Guedes, produced by SPi and premiered last November.

"Inspired (very freely) by a real event, *Rabo de Peixe* tells the fictional story of four friends who see their lives changed with the arrival of a ton of cocaine on the coast of the small Azorean village Rabo de Peixe. The series is a thriller with touches of sarcastic humor and a story based on hope, dreams, friendship, love and the sea that promises to conquer and snatch the audience Portuguese," Netflix said in a statement.
Source: TPN/Lusa

Buyers from 78 countries snapping up Lisbon properties

Foreigners from 78 countries bought 1,655 homes in the Lisbon area alone last year. In 2022, buyers from 78 international nationalities purchased 1,655 houses in the Urban Rehabilitation Area (ARU) of Lisbon, representing an investment amounting to 894.3 million euros, according to data released by *Confidencial Imobiliário*.

Nonetheless, the amount is 7% below the €957.5 million registered in 2021. In terms of the number of properties, the drop is 10%, with 1,845 homes acquired in 2021. The difference in the number of purchasing nationalities is expressive, too, with for 86 countries active in 2021.

French, American, Chinese, British, and Brazilian are the most active nationalities, according to the data.
Source: TPN

Rod Stewart coming to Lisbon

British singer Rod Stewart returns to Portugal in July for a concert in Lisbon filled with his "great hits."

The show by "one of the most successful British musicians ever" is scheduled for July 16 at the Altice Arena. Tickets went on sale on Wednesday, March 29, according to the promoter.

"This will be a concert full of great hits such as 'Forever Young,' 'Can't Stop Me Now,' and 'Do Ya Think I'm Sexy,' among many others."
Source: TPN/Lusa

MEO faces €2.46 million fine

Altice Portugal-owned service provider MEO has been hit with a €2.46 million fine imposed by Portuguese media regulator, Anacom.

The media regulator found MEO had violated the rules applicable to the termination of contracts on the initiative of subscribers.

According to Anacom, MEO did not provide subscribers the termination form that it is obliged to hand over whenever requested, and others in which the company did not ask customers for documents that were necessary to confirm the termination of the respective contracts or requested documents that were not necessary.

On top of this, it found the service provider did not confirm several complaints about contracts submitted

by customers and provided incomplete information on the means and contacts available for submitting termination requests.
Source: Digital TV Europe

End of golden visas threatens €34 million in cultural projects
The end of the golden visa program, one of the measures in the housing crisis package, has halted various investments. Culture is one of the areas affected, with investments of 34 million euros planned for projects related to cinematographic art, according to *Jornal Económico*.

The projects envisaged in this area were mainly concentrated in the interior of the country. There are 170 foreign investors relating to culture, spread over ten projects with a total value of 34 million euros. Clients from the United States, Canada and the Middle East were investing in the country via golden visas.

With the new measures that affect the Residence Permit for Investment Activity regime, some film projects have been suspended. The Ministry of Culture stresses that the topic "is in the legislative process."
Source: TPN

Quinta do Vale Golf Course hosts charity event
What do you get when you combine perfect weather, a golf course designed by the world-famous player Severiano Ballesteros, and a charity that serves both young and old in its community? You get the Charity Event hosted by Quinta do Vale Golf Course on 18 June 2023.

This is the second year Quinta do Vale has hosted this event. The tournament is a better ball-of-partners format using Stableford scoring. You must enter as a pair, and the event is open to anyone with a WHS Index. The entry fee is €140 per team and includes coffee prior to the round, 18 holes of golf, a delicious lunch with wine or beer, a charity auction, and lots of prizes. (Golf carts are available

for €30.) Again this year, money raised will be donated to Santa Casa da Misericórdia de Vila Real de Santo António which has served its community for nearly 100 years. Dedicated to serving the needs of the entire community their services extend from care for infants and preschool children, meal programs for the needy, and in-home care for the elderly. Please enter as a pair via email (golf@quintadovale.com) or call +351 281 531 615.
Source: Press Release

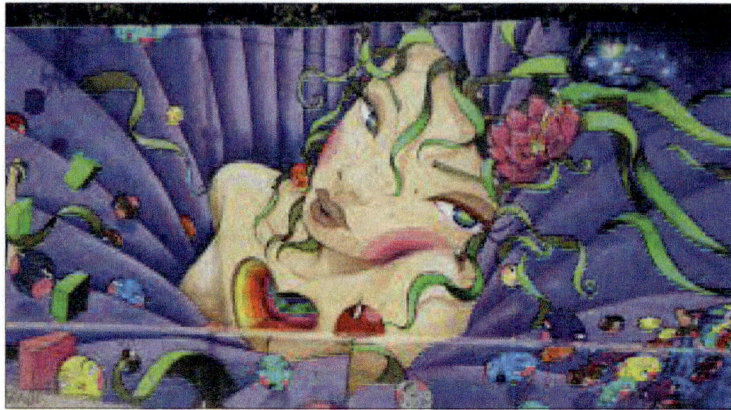

Queer Lisbon LGBTQ history treasure hunt
A new Lisbon tourism experience brought Lisbon's queer history to life through a team adventure in the streets of Bairro Alto and Principe Real on 2 April.

Small teams of approximately five people were given directions and a map to follow, passing gay scene venues and stopping at the sites of Lisbon's fascinating and sometimes bizarre LGBTQ history to answer a list of questions. Three hours later, the small teams came together again in the lounge/ bar/ garden of Late Birds Hotel for a 'pub-quiz' social event and prizes.

Highlights included visiting 17th Century cruising sites and learning how the Inquisition dealt with gay men; lesbians battling 1950s censorship; why Fado is queer; how Pride differs in Portugal; who the 'Three Marias'(and the 'Two Fernandes') were; how LGBT rights were established in Portugal; how the first drag shows started, who the *Principe Real* was; how to see queer films, gay writers, queer pop stars, straight censors, disgraced politicians, trans nuns, real-life spies, 19th Century prostitution, 20th Century feminism—"all this and more as teams found their way around Lisbon's queer neighbourhoods, discovers their history, and end with a party!" explains event organizer Alex Pollard who earned a Master's degree in LGBTQ cultural studies from the University of Sussex (UK) and has been visiting Lisbon for over 30 years. He runs a hiking and culture group in the city and lives in Ajuda.

"I first came to Lisbon in 1989 and fell in love with the city, watching it change as the city grew to embrace tourism and its queer visitors," he adds. "I set up **Lisbon Treasure Hunt Events** to share the stories that I love about the city–not just the major monuments and sites, but social experiences based in the city's locations, with anecdotes and details that bring history alive and opportunities to meet fellow travellers."
Source: Press Release

easyJet announces 27 new summer routes
easyJet will operate 27 new routes in the summer from Portugal, with some of the routes coming from slots it gained from TAP in Lisbon.

"For customers, what matters is more connectivity, more choice and great prices and, therefore, we are really happy to have 27 new routes that we are launching for the next summer season" from Portugal, said easyJet director for the European market, Thomas Haagensen.

Among these routes for the summer aviation season are new direct connections between Lisbon and Bastia (Corsica), Mallorca, Ibiza, Menorca, Barcelona, Birmingham, among others, as well as from Porto to Funchal or to Porto Santo.
Source: TPN/Lusa

TAP airline scandal deepens
Portugal's government fired the chief executive of flag carrier TAP in March 2023 without a legal assessment of the move, Finance Minister Fernando Medina acknowledged, deepening a high-profile scandal around the state-owned airline.

His remarks in parliament contradicted claims by two fellow ministers that the government had obtained a legal opinion backing the decision. This heightens the chances of the state losing a potential lawsuit worth millions of euros by the sacked executives.
Source: Reuters

Jean Paul Gaultier show coming to Portugal
The "Fashion Freak Show", created and directed by and about the French fashion designer Jean Paul Gaultier, will tour Portugal in November, with presentations in Lisbon and Porto.

The "eccentric show of music, fashion and dance", inspired by the life and career of Jean Paul Gaultier, creator of "Madonna's pointed bodices", is presented in Lisbon, in Campo Pequeno, between November 8 and 12, and in Porto, at the Super Bock Arena—Pavilhão Rosa Mota, between 16 and 19 of the same month.

"In this musical celebration, the French designer presents some of his most iconic haute couture pieces, among other models created exclusively for the show, in a setting full of multimedia elements and visual effects", says the promoter.

"The fashion shows and the most important moments in the life of the French 'showman' are recreated, from his childhood to his rise in the world of haute couture, passing through the cultural changes that his fashion mirrored, and his irreverent personality and humorous." Source: TPN/Lusa

When is a building permit needed from the cámara?
Deco explains the existing rules for undertaking basic building works in a report by idealista.

Authorization from the city council is not required when:

Works do not require demolition, which therefore do not jeopardize the stability of the property or the building (does not affect pillars, beams or support walls), or do not involve modifying the height of the house or its floors, or the shape of the facades or the roof. However, Deco advises that you still should always consult a technician. In the case of a building, a notice of works must be placed;

Painting the house (apartment) inside or tiling in kitchens or bathrooms;

Fixing the roof or installing solar panels—if, at the end of the work, the roof is in an identical location and the solar panels do not exceed the coverage area of the building nor exceed its height by one meter;

Closing off a balcony—in many municipalities it is mandatory to have a municipal license, but in others it is enough to make prior communication with the council. Check with your municipality. In the case of a building in a condominium, and since the architectural line of the building may be at stake, the condominium must authorize the work by a two-thirds majority. The same is valid for placing protections on balconies.

Authorization from the city council is required when:

Modifying the facade of the building, enlarging it, for example, implies municipal licensing;

Painting the building a different color than the original (painting the same tone does not require formalities). Source: Idealista

Online residency renewals
Approximately 25,000 foreigners residing in Portugal whose residence permits expire by 30 June can renew the document automatically through the SEF website.

The Foreigners and Borders Service (SEF) states that around 25,000 foreigners can automatically renew their residence permits (AR) using the Automatic Renewal feature, available in the "Personal Area" of the portal.

According to SEF, the Automatic Renewal functionality is part of the simplification of procedures, whereby there is no need to visit a service desk in person, ensuring "compliance with safety rules and mitigation of the consequences that resulted from the situation of health emergency."

This measure of automatically renewing residence permits, which lasts for two years, came about in July 2020 due to the covid-19 pandemic, with more than 200,000 automatic renewals having been carried out.

"The service has been adopting exceptional measures, with a view to recovering pending issues and ensuring efficiency in the document management of foreign citizens, following Order No. 5793-A/2020 of May 22, 2020, which determined the implementation of a procedure simplified processing of applications for granting a residence permit."

SEF also indicates that, among the initiatives to mitigate the consequences resulting from the pandemic, the automatic renewal of residence permits is the one that has had the greatest impact and has allowed "the recovery of pending issues and a gain in efficiency in the document management of foreign citizens." Source: TPN/Lusa

Ageing population in Portugal
Portugal has a fertility rate of 1.4, a number below the necessary value of 2.1 for the replacement of generations, according to the report of the United Nations Population Fund (UNFPA).

The report shows that 23% of the Portuguese are over 65 years old and 38% are in the age group from zero to 24

Let the Alentejo embrace you. Stay in style.

"Among the best in Portugal"
boa cama boa mesa Expresso

ASSUMAR COUNTRY HOUSE
RUA DE CABEÇO DE VIDE 17 ASSUMAR
WWW.ASSUMARCOUNTRYHOUSE.COM

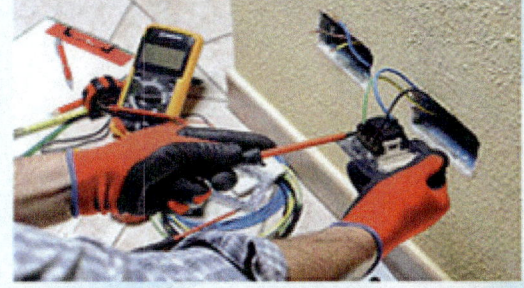

Francisco J.O. Silva
Certified **Electrician** & **Plumber**

Climate Control · Home Automation Systems
Solar Heating & Domestic Hot Water · Plumbing
Thermal Solar & Photovoltaic Energy · Electricity

CONTACT US!
We will be glad to help you!
We use WhatsApp & speak english

✉ franciscojosilva@gmail.com

📞 00351 919 333 948

[f] [ig]

What our clients say about our services

"Not only did Francisco do a fantastic job on both our electrical and plumbing needs, but his work was fastidious, within our budget, and completed on time." **Bruce Joffe and Russ Warren (Alcains)**

"Francisco was reliable and simply amazing at his job. Nothing is too much trouble for him and an added bonus is that he is so friendly. I cannot recommend this man highly enough." **Peter Singh (Fundão)**

years old. The United Nations report accounts for 64% of Portuguese aged between 15 and 24 years.

UNFPA notes that average global life expectancy reached 72.8 years in 2019, an increase of nearly nine years since 1990, and is expected to reach 77.2 years by 2050, after accounting for the effects of the COVID-19 pandemic. In Portugal, the average life expectancy is 85 years for women and 80 years for men.
Source: TPN/Lusa

Countries with Europe's most homeowners
Portugal is a country of landlords, with the culture of owning a home more common than being that of a tenant.

According to Landgeist.com, which relies on Eurostat data, the number of homeowners varies greatly from country to country, with the option to buy a home more common in Eastern Europe than in Western Europe.

Fewer homeowners are in Spain, Italy, and France than in Portugal, the percentage being 75.8%, 73.7%, and 64.7%, respectively.

In the opposite direction are Austria, Germany, and Switzerland, which are the European countries where there are more tenants than homeowners. In the specific case of Germany and Switzerland there are more people renting houses than buying.
Source: TPN

EDP to lower electricity prices
Electricity prices will drop in the second half of this year, according to the CEO of EDP, Miguel Stilwell de Andrade, who, in an interview with Expresso, underlines that the Portuguese electricity company has always sought to have "competitive prices," despite competing companies charging lower values.

Miguel Stilwell de Andrade warns that the price reduction "will depend on access tariffs," but that in the energy component "it will still be a relevant reduction" that "could reach double digits." But the price reduction will also be felt in gas which, after having shot up last year, "has been experiencing a reduction" which will also be reflected "in prices for consumers in Portugal."
Source: The Portugal News

Buy or rent in Portugal this year?
Moving to Portugal is a dizzying dream for many. If you're looking to make that dream a reality in 2023, you're by no means alone. Portugal remains one of the most popular destinations for expats leaving the United Kingdom, the US, and many other countries around the world.

But the big question for most expats landing on Portugal's shores is whether they should buy or rent their new home.

While it may seem like a simple question for many, there are several factors to consider, particularly given the

28   Portugal Living Magazine

Comprehensive Services Include:

- Inspect periodically the property granting that it is maintained in good conditions
- Setting up and adhering to budgets for property maintenance
- Arranging for necessary repairs to properties
- Rent Collection and transfer to landlord bank account in 5 working days
- Issue the receipt in Finanças Portal and handling taxes
- Understanding national landlord-tenant laws and regulations
- Presence on HOA meetings

927 068 077

HELLO@TIAGOFREITAS.PT

current social and political climate in Portugal and the world at large. So, before you make your decision, here are a few things to bear in mind when deciding if you should buy or rent a home in Portugal in 2023.

Sky High Prices

The aftermath of the COVID-19 pandemic, the uncertainty of the war in Ukraine, and various other factors have led to towering interest rates and inflation. While this isn't only true of Portugal, the Portuguese housing market is currently booming. With a huge amount of foreign investment in recent years, thanks to programs like the Golden Visa, house prices have been rising at an astonishing rate. A combination of this and the current inflation situation means that, if you are purchasing a property in Portugal right now, you're going to pay a lot for it.

Considering the recent announcement that the Golden Visa is coming to an end, and the fact that economies are—as a whole—starting to right themselves following all the upheaval, it seems likely that house prices in Portugal are about to drop, making it a poor time to invest in the property market.

Renting a home while you wait for house prices to drop may ultimately prove to be a cheaper option than losing a huge chunk of the value of your new property. This is particularly true if a house purchase would tie you into current interest rates, which are staggeringly high.

A drop in market value is always the gamble we take when investing in the housing market; but given the current socio-economic climate in Portugal—not to mention the rest of Europe and beyond—it's an even more important factor to consider this year.

Buying vs Renting for The Digital Nomad

While the Golden Visa may have come to an end, the Digital Nomad Visa is going strong. Those taking advantage of this scheme, to live in the country for a year or two, may be better off renting to avoid all the stress, paperwork, and charges that come with buying a house.

The flip side to this is if you plan to retain the property once you've left residency. You may have plans for a holiday home to return to once your visa expires or to renovate and resell while in residence to earn money on the sale.

For potential holiday homeowners, it's important to be aware that the government has recently banned new rental licenses for Airbnb and other short-term rentals. This was done to ensure more affordable housing for locals but may make it tough to rent your property in the months you are absent, once you're no longer in permanent residence.

Financing Considerations

The other obvious factor to consider is your current financial situation. Before deciding to buy a house in Portugal, consider your income; is it guaranteed or unpredictable? If you're confident you'll be able to make your mortgage repayment on time, consider your effort rate: generally, this should not exceed 35% if you're looking to buy. When making this calculation, don't forget to factor in all credit expenses, not just your potential mortgage.

If you decide to go ahead, your next hurdle will be your deposit. While it's natural to face this issue on any house purchase, you're very unlikely to get a bank to lend you more than 90% of the value of your house. Realistically, you may be looking at only 80%, and considerably less for non-residents. Can you comfortably afford the deposit required?

You will also need to factor in the costs associated with your purchase. This includes stamp duty, the deed and registration of the house, and council tax.
Source: Blacktower in The Portugal News

Sharon Stone joins George Clooney in Portugal
The 65-year-old actress has acquired land at the Costa Terra Golf & Ocean Club development in Melides in the Alentejo. This information about the Hollywood star was revealed by commentator Rui Oliveira (husband of Manuel Luís Goucha) and Maya on the CMTV program "Noite das Estrelas."

"There is another actress who is going to move to Portugal," revealed Rui. "This time it is Sharon Stone who is coming to Portugal, to be neighbors with Manuel Luís Goucha, Rui Oliveira, and George Clooney. With the house being built in the Melides area," said Maya.

According to Adriano Silva Martins and other commentators on the CMTV program, the property

This artwork was curated by M.A.S.C.—Movimento os Amigos de São Cristóvão. They thought of the amazing historical and cultural value of this part of Lisbon and felt compelled to show it to everyone. They gathered funds by offering fado to the neighborhood, as a street party with traditional food and drinks. The result of several artists' works can be seen on the Escadinhas de São Cristóvão.
Source: VisitLisboa.com

Photo Credit: josefmagalhaes

cost around ten million euros and is already under construction at the Costa Terra Golf & Ocean Club estate.

That 200-hectare development is owned by the American company Discovery Land Company and the minimum price for a lot currently is 3.4 million euros. The project includes 292 homes and a golf course designed by Tom Fazio.

In addition to being neighbors with Portuguese personalities, Sharon Stone will live very close to George Clooney who has also bought land at the Costa Terra Golf & Ocean Club.
Source: TPN

Electric car support fund already empty
According to *Jornal de Notícias*, 1,348 requests for reimbursements have been made since March, however there was a limit of only 1,300 incentives granted by the Environmental Fund.

Applications already exceed the limit of incentives to be granted by the government, with 1,348 requests for reimbursement being filed since March, says the *Jornal*.

Of the 1,348 applications for support of €4,000 per beneficiary in the purchase of electric vehicles, made available by the Environmental Fund, 255 are approved, 1,053 are under analysis and five have been excluded. This means that if all the candidates under analysis are approved, 43 may not receive any support.

Questioned about a possible increase in funds, the Ministry of the Environment told *Jornal de Notícias* that "the evaluation of applications for support of 10 million euros for the acquisition of electric and smooth mobility vehicles is still ongoing, so the procedure regarding incentives has not yet been closed." Applications for the purchase of scooters, skateboards, hoverboards, skates, monowheels, tricycles and light quadricycles have also exceeded the 1,050 allowed.
Source: TPN

Accommodation revenues surpassed €5 billion last year

Revenues of over €5 billion euros were registered in hotel establishments in Portugal last year, accounting for an increase of more than 114.6 per cent compared to the previous year.

Such conclusions have been reached by the recent report of the DBK Informa, SchengenVisaInfo.com reports.

The study revealed that in Portugal's hotel sector, the value reached last year surpassed by 16.5 per cent what had been registered before the spread of the coronavirus and its new strains in 2019.

In addition, the study, which also included hotels as well as local accommodation units, tourist apartments, apart-hotels, as well as tourism establishments, revealed that last year also registered an increase in the number of visitors and overnight stays, compared to 2021 figures.

"Local accommodation establishments were the ones that showed the highest percentage growth in the number of guests, while in overnight stays, the biggest growth corresponded to hotels," the report noted, stressing that this type of accommodation saw the highest number of guests.

The survey revealed that national tourists accounted for nearly 23 million overnight stays, about a third of the total and a total of 23 per cent more compared to 2021, while the rest of the overnight stays were from international tourists, accounting for a growth of 150 per cent.

"Among foreigners, the biggest increases were registered among residents of the United States (+327 per cent), Brazil (+265 per cent), and the United Kingdom (+192 per cent). The British remained the most important foreign customers, representing 13 per cent of overnight stays, ahead of Germans and Spaniards," the study revealed.
Source: Schengenvisa

Portugal must apologize, be held accountable for colonization

Portugal must apologize and assume responsibility for the exploitation and slavery during the colonial period, President Marcelo Rebelo de Sousa said in a speech following Brazilian President Lula da Silva's state visit in April.

De Sousa took this position in his speech at the commemorative session of the 49th anniversary of the April 25 Revolution, commemorating a military coup in 1974 that ended the dictatorial Estado Novo regime and initiated the decolonization of Portuguese colonies.

"This is also useful for us to look back about Brazil. But it would also be possible for all colonization and all decolonization, and for us to take full responsibility for what we did," he said.

"It's not just saying sorry—which is undoubtedly due—for what we did because saying sorry is sometimes the easiest thing to do: you say sorry, turn your back, and the job is done. No, it is the assumption of responsibility for the future of the good and bad things we did in the past," he added.

According to de Sousa, the colonization of Brazil also had positive factors, "the language, the culture, the unity of the Brazilian territory. Of the bad, the exploitation of the original peoples, denounced by António Vieira, slavery, the sacrifice of the interests of Brazil and Brazilians," he pointed out.

The president of Portugal also left a message of condemnation to those who are "selfish in the face of the dramas of the immigrants."
Source: Euractiv

image: eBay

Let's Talk Money

By Sarah Davie

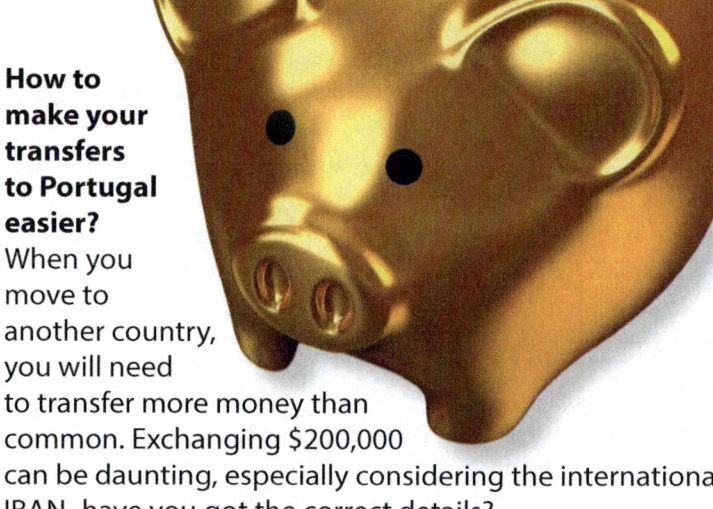

When planning your move to Portugal, there is a lot to consider, especially in terms of your finances.

Typically, the main costs involve visas and accommodation. For example, you will need to consider:

- Visa costs
- Legal fees
- Paying for a NIF
- Rental payments or property purchase costs
- Removal and Relocation fees

Then, the miscellaneous that often get forgotten about when you come over on your scouting trips or finally make the move.

- Flights
- Hotels/ AirBnb
- Furnishings for your rental or property
- Moving savings/money to live on
- Car purchase
- Groceries
- Eating out
- Utilities

The difference in costs can be a few €'s here or there, or a couple of hundred. But it could even be a few thousand! You are adding up the euro amounts and calculating the cost in US Dollars, Pounds, or Canadian Dollars (whatever currency you use in your home country) on a specific day. If you make those calculations on another day—or when you are making those payments—the amounts could be vastly different.

Traditionally, your bank would be your first port of call. However, it is always worth checking the exchange rate. We usually see a 3-4% difference between banks and overseas financial specialists.

How to make your transfers to Portugal easier?

When you move to another country, you will need to transfer more money than common. Exchanging $200,000 can be daunting, especially considering the international IBAN–have you got the correct details?

Consider using a currency specialist in the same way you would use a financial advisor. They are experts in this field.

How to control the cost of my transfers?

1. **Buy euros in advance**
   You do not need a Portuguese euro account to take advantage of this option. There is no minimum, and Spartan FX can hold your funds on account free of charge.

2. **Splitting your transfers**
   Splitting your payments means that if the rate moves against you, the average rate at which you will have bought your Euros will be better.

   For example, suppose you bought €200,000 and split your payments in half. Based on a EUR/USD rate, this is purely an example:

   - Half at 1.10 and if the rate moves against you, half at 1.20. The average is 1.15
   - Half at 1.10 and if the rate moves against you, half at parity. The average is 1.05

Bank Comparison	Cost of buying €200,000*	Difference
US Bank	$219.058	
Spartan FX (Currency Specialist)	$213,447	$5,611

*based on an exchange rate on 15/12/22 against Wells Fargo

3. **Monitor the rate and plan ahead**
   Think about these transfers before you make them. The more time you give yourself, the more options you will have. Your personal currency expert can help to monitor the rate of exchange for you, leaving you time to focus on the rest of your move.

By advance planning, you could save money and make the process easier for yourself.

- How will you move your money when you are no longer in the USA/UK/Canada etc, and you are staying or living in Portugal?
- Does your bank have limits on how much you can transfer?
- Do you need to sign any paperwork or order an international card reader in advance?

Researching and asking these questions early on can make the process of transferring your money easier and less hassle.

The Chilli Experience have one of the largest selections of spices, spice mixes, dried herbs and chillies available for immediate despatch across the whole of Portugal

In season, we also have a full range of chilli plants (collection only) and fresh chillies for sale that are grown on our Chilli Farm in Central Portugal

Order online at:

www.thechilliexperience.com

Specialist Suppliers of:

Dried Herbs

Whole Spices

Ground Spices

Indian Curry Mixes

BBQ Rubs

Tex-Mex Seasoning

Middle Eastern Spice Mixes

Dried Chillies

Chilli Seeds

Fresh Chillies (in Season)

Chilli Plants (April/May)

Spartan FX is an award-winning currency specialist that's helped hundreds of customers save time and money on their overseas transfers and enabled them to achieve their dream of moving to Portugal. Our experts Ben Amrany, **Sarah Davie**, and Neil Poyton regularly share money-saving tips on expat community webinars in Portugal.

33 Portugal Living Magazine

Selling Portugal

By Bruce H. Joffe

Portugal is currently home to around seven thousand Americans and it would seem that demand for the small, westernmost southern European country from North America is only gaining traction.

Do you have any idea how many Americans from the USA (alone) are moving to Portugal in increasing numbers?

Enough to command cover stories and feature articles from Condé Nast Traveler, Político, The Los Angeles Times, CNN, and many others.

The Wall Street Journal stated that Americans are retiring to Portugal "in droves," attracted by "a low cost of living, healthcare, a sunny climate, and tax incentives," while Forbes crowed that, "Portugal has seen a surge of popularity in recent years for expatriates seeking to move their nest for a better life. Whether it's Lisbon, Porto, the Azores, Algarve, or further inland, this country of diverse landscape has somewhere for everyone.

Over our five years living in Portugal, we've seen a lot of hype and disinformation spread about the country. For us and many others, it's a great place to live. But too many people get caught up in all the hype and the hoopla: How many different international media and magazines have already decreed that Portugal is the top place to be … to visit … to live … to eat … to drink wine … to retire?

With well over 100,000 members, the largest Facebook group for expats and immigrants in Portugal is Moving to Portugal. More than 250 people seek to join this caravan every day!

Truth be told, Portugal is being oversold.

I suspect that many professionals who can't find appropriate work (and pay) in the country are pumping up the rhetoric and joining the bandwagon of those selling Portugal. Grocers specializing in food products generally hard to find are shipping them to your doorstep in Portugal. Therapists are dealing with post-expatric syndrome and a host of other unsettling behaviors. Lawyers are catering to the big slice of business that comprises the market of people needing NIFs, bank accounts, and houses. Property agencies are a dime a dozen. Relocation experts promise to facilitate the transition. Packed tighter than sardines in a tin are webinars, blogs, vlogs, and YouTube channels catering to expats, immigrants, and foreigners. We have countless scores of people and groups teaching Portuguese in a variety of formats. Others are arranging round-trip scouting trips to the destination(s) of client interest(s), as well as charter flights bringing people and their pets to Portugal. Customized trips and tours are at your disposal, as are money lenders and currency brokers. Portugal itself is subsidizing numerous public relations undertakings that lure people—as tourists, travelers, and residents—to its land of the fado and saudade.

Still, there's a point to be realistic and not conjure up expectations of cobble stone streets with Porto flowing freely. It just doesn't work that way.

"The sales gimmick of Portugal having the best beaches in Europe, the warm weather, low cost of living, and hospitable people was charming and very appealing. However, as reality set in, I discovered a different picture—more of a western country being operated as a third world country, or an eastern bloc bureaucratic central system," one critic said.

Like everywhere these days, Portugal—and the European Union—has its share of liberals and alt-righters. There are robberies, both burglaries and advantage-taking. Not everyone is nice; some people are downright nasty. Fuel is more expensive here, at least three times its cost in the USA. It gets bone-chilling cold all over the country, a different type of cold that we've not experienced elsewhere. There's mold and bugs and flies and creepy crawlers. And lots of houses that continue to be inhabited since they were built (and hardly upgraded) in the 1930s, 40s, and 50s. Yes, there are some people who have different attitudes about domestic pets than we do. We cringe when we hear of their abuse and abandonment. They may cringe when they see us treating our dogs and cats as children, rather than pets. But increasingly, I see Portuguese people walking their dogs on leads, picking up after them, buying specialty foods at upscale pet shops, and taking their "familiars" to the vet to be diagnosed, treated, and inoculated.

My friend João (don't we all have at least one?), whom I respect immensely, responded to a litany of complaints about living in Portugal with these words:

"We describe things as we are, not as they are. As objective as one can be, the overall joy of living in one place cannot be calculated from some parameters on a bullet list. I must say that as a former expat myself, what some considered negative points were truly the things that made me happy. Take into consideration that the grass is always greener … and there will always be people (seeking to) overrate their products—countries included."

One of the questions asked of would-be members to Moving to Portugal, the largest Facebook group for expats, immigrants, and others interested in moving to Portugal is "What do you like most about Portugal?" By far, the majority of those answering say "Everything!"

Give me a break, please. Most of them have yet to set foot in the country, but they already know that they like everything about Portugal. Yeah, right.

A friend, Rudi, posted this on her Facebook feed today: "I love my little village. I spent this morning emailing and calling four companies to ask if they could send me an invoice for work they had done at my place and materials they had delivered. After four texts from me, the wood guy finally did send me an invoice for wood he delivered the first week of October. I don't think I ever before had to beg to pay my bills."

That's the paradox of Portugal.

For some reason, I'm reminded of these lyrics from Joni Mitchell's Big Yellow Taxi: "They paved paradise and put up a parking lot."

Those who come to Portugal because they've been sold on it being paradise are in for some surprises and reality checks. Just what is "paradise," anyway? One person's paradise may put another in the doldrums.

For yours truly, it's living in peace—safely and securely. It's having a diverse group of multilingual friends who enjoy being together. It's marveling at the splendors of the world within driving distance. It's integrating into the culture rather than making it subordinate to ours.

"There are much cheaper places to retire than Portugal and too many Americans have come with unrealistic expectations," says my friend Nancy, a blogger living now in Portugal. "And while the cost of living may be at parity with the USA, the feeling of peace, and the joy of new experiences nearly every day are priceless."

We experience that in Portugal.

"At the end it's a wonderful country to experience but it's not paradise," commented Jon Collier in a post. "That's a place you create in your heart."

An American who emigrated from the USA after Trump's inauguration in 2017, Bruce Joffe is publisher and creative director of *Portugal Living Magazine*, the "thoughtful magazine for people everywhere with Portugal on their minds."

35 Portugal Living Magazine

What I've Learned to Accept ...
... but still occasionally confuses or confounds me

By Beth Thomas-Kim

Moving to another country is exciting. Everything is new and unusual, which can be both stimulating and fun, but also confusing and frustrating at times.

However, after three years, much of that has become familiar and less stressful. The Euro no longer feels like play money. I can quickly discern between a 5, 10, and 20 Euro bill.

Of course, learning the language is an ongoing effort. I have become familiar with many words, especially when they are written like the ones mentioning promotions and discounts in store windows. Thankfully, we have learned the majority of traffic signs and directions, like when to turn on the car headlamps, moderate our speed when it's raining, and reminders to maintain a safe distance from the car in front of us.

Beth's dog, Sweet Pea

Unfortunately, spoken language can still confuse me, especially if I'm worried or stressed. Just this week we needed to take Sweet Pea to the 24-hour emergency vet. It was around 9PM when I called, and it went to a recorded message. The first message was provided in both Portuguese and English (my call was important, and it would be answered as soon as possible); however, while I was waiting it shifted to another message that I did not understand and then the line was automatically disconnected.

Thankfully, we have used this vet clinic in the past and I know they have a technology that allows them to see that someone has called and will proactively call them back quickly even if a message wasn't left. This was the case for me. We are grateful that everyone at the clinic speaks English so we can easily communicate our concerns about Sweet Pea. (Just in case you are wondering, she will be 15 this year and her health is becoming more fragile. We were able to immediately get her on some medication and she is beginning to feel better.)

Time, practice, context, surroundings, repetitiveness, and patience have helped us to feel comfortable living here.

And while so much has become familiar, there are unique aspects of Portugal that still make me scratch my head in disbelief or cause me to laugh out loud, but mostly not to question any more.

Let's start with how the floors in buildings are numbered. In the US all ground floors are known as number one, the *first* floor. That makes perfect sense to me. Unfortunately, it is not the case here.

While I give the Europeans major props for fully embracing roundabouts, small cars, compact living, and the metric system, which is logically *far superior* to the crazy Imperial system, the numbering mechanism in buildings doesn't make sense to me. Here, ground floors are considered 0. Will someone explain where the logic is in that?

Oh, don't bother. It's not like it's going to change.

Here's another oddity. In Portugal, there is a unique greeting for specific times of the day, but there is no generic greeting that covers the entire day. In the US, the term "good day" can be used until the sun sets and sometimes even after that. In Portugal, from dawn until 11:59AM, people say *bom dia*, which literally means good day. However, beginning at noon, you immediately switch to *boa tarde* (good afternoon).

When to stop saying *boa tarde* is a little less clear. Everyone we have asked has given us a different answer on when to switch to *boa noite* (good night).

Some of you probably noted that good day uses "*bom*" while good afternoon and good night use "*boa*." Both words mean good. However, the word *dia* is considered masculine while *tarde* and *noite* are feminine which is why they have different spellings. Every noun in Portuguese is either masculine or feminine. You just have to learn them all.

Another "fun" aspect of feminine and masculine differences in the language is that if there are 999 women in a group and one male, the masculine pronoun is used.

Something that makes me laugh out loud are the local church bells. I love to hear them ringing throughout the day and evening. Unfortunately, it's best not to rely on them to note the time. Last week, I heard them on various days ringing at 10:13 AM, 2.24 PM, and 7:41 PM ... and they didn't necessarily chime the correct number of the closest hour, half hour, or even quarter hour. I'm not sure why this is. I envision an older gentleman who slowly climbs to the top of the bell tower and starts to pull the rope whenever he gets there, pulling it as many times as he has the time, interest, or strength for.

Another oddity is a rather dangerous one: stop signs. People see them either as a suggestion or not at all. I have a few theories on this. One is that people park their cars right up to the edge of the intersection requiring all traffic signs to be positioned high enough to be seen over cars, vans, and trucks of all heights. Because the traffic signs are positioned so high, they are not in the line of sight of a driver. And guess what? There are accidents as a result. We have personally witnessed four such accidents at the intersection near our house. Thankfully, none were serious. Naturally, this makes us especially careful at all intersections when we're driving or even walking.

We have also come to resign ourselves to the inconsistent service of the national postal service called CTT. Sometimes they are great—they proactively send you an email or text message informing you of an impending delivery along with a timeframe in which you can expect it. There are times when it works perfectly.

Then there are the days when you receive those messages, dutifully stay home ALL DAY, and then get a message later saying the attempted delivery was unsuccessful because no one was home. *Grrrrrr…..*

When that happens, we have to schlepp down to the local CTT office, get a number (which is typically 20-30 numbers behind the current number being served) in order to get our package. I don't know if this odd service extreme has something to do with CTT having been established in 1520 imbuing their employees with a sense of "you'll get it when you get it." It's pretty obvious they aren't going out of business any time soon. On the plus side, they do have the cutest little delivery vehicles and not all our packages are delivered via CTT. *Whew!*

Even though some situations still get me riled up, for the most part we take all the oddities in stride and try to have a good sense of humor about them. Mostly we just learn to adapt. Overall, those minor irritations just make living here that much more interesting.

After working in corporate America for companies like Mattel, Nestlé, and Johnson & Johnson, Beth retired and moved to Portugal in January of 2020 with her husband, Won, and their 12-year old wire fox terrier, Sweet Pea. Beth's blog was started to keep family and friends updated on their transition from the USA to Portugal. Now, subscribers include people from all over the world.

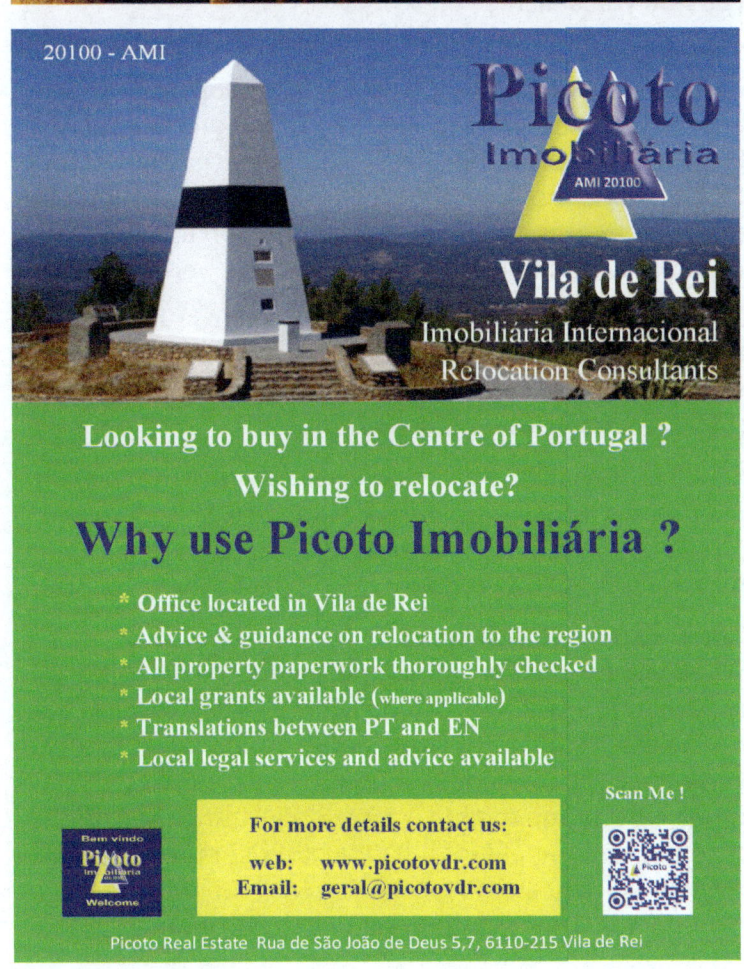

37 Portugal Living Magazine

Minding Your Manners
Unspoken Portuguese Rules of Etiquette
By Carol A. Wilcox

Do you often wonder if you're using the correct word or phrase when speaking to a Portuguese person? Are you hoping that you don't make an embarrassing faux pas by misusing a specific form of address or gesture to someone, especially in a professional setting?

When you're just learning the lingo and adjusting to a new culture, you may be making unintentional errors. I know I have. Portugal still practices a good deal of formality in both professional and daily living. And while most Portuguese are friendly, there's still a conservative, unspoken protocol on the proper way to address someone.

Based on a reader's comment on my post, *Dazed and Confused in Portugal*, I decided to delve into some of the more common unspoken Portuguese rules of etiquette. Use this information as a guideline only. It's important to understand that these are unspoken rules and as such, your experiences may vary depending on the situation you find yourself in.

Saying 'hello.'
I have been listening (*really* paying attention) to how people greet me in Portuguese. From the grocery delivery person, the letter carrier, the laundry service person, the cashier at the mercado, the Uber driver, the receptionist at the doctor's office, to the person getting off the elevator I'm patiently waiting for, are all polite, reservedly friendly, and generally say the following to me:

Hello, good morning = *Olá, bom dia*.
Hello, good afternoon = *Olá, boa tarde*.
Hello, good evening = *Olá, boa noite*.

Some abbreviate the greeting by eliminating the *Olá*, but most I have noticed use the whole phrase. So that's what I try to use (I think it's safe to do this, plus it does sound nice as it rolls off my tongue).

When you meet and greet.
When you meet a Portuguese person for the first time, especially in a business setting, your greeting should be polite and sincere. It is customary to use direct eye contact and shake hands (or now in Covid/post-Covid times, a fist bump might be preferable), using the 'hello' greeting appropriate for the time of day. At the end of your meeting or as you are leaving, you should shake hands again. This applies to both men and women.

For people you know, such as friends or acquaintances, it is common for men to shake hands and give one another a pat on the back. Women may be greeted with a light kiss (or 'air kiss') on each cheek, starting with the right cheek. I have personally been greeted by both Portuguese men and women—friends and acquaintances—this way (although I'm still getting used to which cheek goes first).

Social settings.
If you're invited to a party or, perhaps, dinner with a group of people, it is customary to greet each person who arrived before you. When leaving, it is customary to say goodbye to each person before you head out.

On being friendly to strangers.
If we're walking along a neighborhood sidewalk in Portugal, most people will walk right past us without so much as a nod. I don't think it's rudeness … but I do think it's the custom as I discovered while researching this topic. Greeting strangers you pass in a small village setting is appropriate. Greeting strangers as you walk in a larger town or city is not.

Sometimes, however, a person will surprise us with a smile or nod or even an *Olá*. So, many of these nuances I'm describing here are not necessarily carved in stone.

Senhor, senhora, or something else?
Portugal has a long-standing culture of hierarchy which means that position, age, and authority are respected. People in senior positions should always be addressed formally both in oral and written communication.

The use of *senhor* or *cavaleiro* ('the gentleman') and *senhora* or *dona* ('the lady') are titles of honor and can be used in formal situations, or to respectfully address older Portuguese folks. It can also be used to emphasize respect such as when addressing someone in law enforcement, academia, or government. Senhor/senhora can also mean sir/madam or Mr./Mrs./Ms.

Portuguese people will use first names as a form of address to friends, children, and teenagers. In other situations, it is customary to address adults by their title and surname. You should not assume a first name only basis until you are invited to do so (especially in a formal or business setting).

Doutor or doutora—who and why?
There seems to be some confusion regarding the proper way to address someone with a university degree—be it

medical or educational. I found this resource that breaks it down somewhat clearly:

Doutor is the masculine word in Portuguese for doctor. The abbreviation is Dr.

Doutora is the feminine word in Portuguese for doctor. The abbreviation is Dra.

In academia, *doutor/doutora* is used for people who have completed a university doctorate.

In medicine, *doutor/doutora* is used for people who have graduated from a university of medicine.

Doutor/doutora can refer to someone who is knowledgeable and cultured. The term can also indicate a title of someone with authority in the judiciary system, as well as or one who is deserving of respectful treatment.

Individuals with a university degree can be addressed using the title of honor (*senhor/senhora*) plus *doutor/doutora* with or without their surname or first name.

The abbreviation *PhD* is not used to indicate the degree of doctor or doctorate in Portugal.

Portugal, like other Latin countries, is more relaxed about time. If you're from somewhere else (such as the U.S.), you may find this to be a difficult adjustment (but adjusting will probably be better overall for your health). In Portugal, it is acceptable to be a few minutes late for an appointment or meeting (maybe 10-15 minutes at the most). Deadlines are not as critical as with other cultures. Follow-through may not be at the speed you're accustomed to.

It's also good to remember that if you're planning to make appointments or schedule a business meeting in Portugal, the month of August and the weeks leading up to Christmas and New Year are considered holiday periods, so you likely won't get too much response. Ditto for Good Friday through Easter Sunday.

Go with the flow and plan accordingly.

The one phrase to learn and remember.
Most people Paul and I have encountered in Portugal are very tolerant and forgiving, especially if you make an unspoken etiquette mistake. Practice saying the phrase, '*desculpe-me*' which means, '*I'm sorry*' in Portuguese. Acknowledging a faux pas and apologizing for it can go a long way.

Carol writes the Our Portugal Journey blog. Her excellent perceptions and interpretations of an American couple's discoveries, challenges, and experiences in moving to and living in Portugal are also posted on Facebook.

GIN SCHOOL EXPERIENCE
Porto, Portugal

€85.00 (incl IVA) price valid to 31/12/23

Duration: 3 hours approx.

Included in your INVICTA GIN SCHOOL Experience

- Distilling introduction and Q&A,
- 3 x Gin & Tonics (spread across your experience)
- Choosing and blending botanicals to create your own unique Gin
- Distilling, bottling, labelling and naming your own Gin creation
- A personal cheese and bread tabua

@invictaginschool

www.scoundrelsdistilling.com

Praça da Corujeira 158 Porto, 4300-144

CANNABIS: health education & products

Learn how non-psychoactive cannabis may be the answer you're looking for

CBD and other cannabis compounds can have an incredible effect on our health.

WE RUN: online educational webinars
OUR HISTORY: pioneers of the CBD industry over a decade ago
And still providing the ONLY oils in the world listed in the Physicians' Desk Reference

Fully legal in Portugal and throughout Europe

If you are interested in understanding more about this powerful yet misunderstood plant, email Dan for details.

Dan Marshall / dan@helpmetohemp.com / 911 082 930

Portugal Living Magazine

Expat Attorneys in Portugal
Representing You and Your Rights

By Bruce H. Joffe

My temporary residência is expired. But it's impossible to get in touch with SEF. What should I do? Can you help me?

I'm not working with a property agent or agency. If I find a house I want to buy, can you write the contract and represent me?

After closing on the property I purchased, I discovered that the seller(s) violated some of the terms of the contract—taking items they were supposed to leave and leaving stuff they were supposed to take. Do I have legal recourse?

Do you represent expats and immigrants in domestic affairs?

The contractor I hired isn't fulfilling his responsibilities according to the contract—in Portuguese—that he wrote. A neighbor translated it for me because I don't understand Portuguese that well yet. Whom should I turn to for help?

These, among many others, are questions that Portuguese lawyers are asked. But attorneys working with expats and immigrants are involved in so much more—often beginning with the purchase of property.

Ask for recommendations for legal services and—depending upon the group you're asking—two names are bound to come up: **Liliana Solipa** and **Rosário Vital**. Gracious and experienced, their professional services do us justice.

Sole practitioner **Liliana** received her five-year law degree from Coimbra University in 2004 and has been practicing since 2005. Her practice includes property, family and minor, and criminal law.

"I deal with almost everything," she says, except for working with the administrative and fiscal court.

Liliana's clients are both Portuguese and foreign—she speaks English, French, and Spanish—dealing with court filings as well as the purchase and sale of properties. A typical day includes meeting with clients at her office, processing deeds, and sessions at court.

What does she like most—and least—about her work? "Waiting for answers from public services" is the most frustrating aspect of her work, while "achieving the results clients want" is the most satisfying.

"Get accurate information from a professional," she advises, "because there is too much incorrect information online—especially since no two situations are the same."

On Mother's Day 2020, husband Nuno Carneiro posted this about her on Facebook:

"Lawyer, friend, teacher, child, adviser, kind, tireless, educator, and above all mother … (you're the) incredible woman I had the privilege of bumping into, building a life with and wonderful family. I could spend all day writing about you; there wouldn't be enough space or characters to describe what an extraordinary person you are … let me just say what a privilege it is to be by your side every day."

Originally from Santarém, **Rosário** now lives and practices law in Lisbon. A dual citizen of the USA and Portugal, she's a Portuguese-accredited lawyer with over 20 years of experience—15 in a multinational context—who serves as legal coordinator for Relocator Portugal, of which she is sole proprietor.

Earning her five-year law degree from the Law University of Lisbon, Rosário continued her legal studies after graduation at the Law University of Coimbra. "My transcripts have been recognized by WES (World Education Services in New York), one of the most accredited foreign evaluation transcript agencies in the USA," she says with pride. "It was the equivalent to a master's degree in law."

Today, Rosário specializes in real estate law, immigration, and inheritance law. Like Liliana, Rosário says, "I don't deal directly with criminal and labor law but have people on my team who can assist with those matters."

Rosário works primarily—by choice—with the USA market; less than five percent of her clients are from countries outside the USA.

"I get great satisfaction and happiness from being a part of helping people fulfill their dreams and ambitions," she beams. "This encourages me to try my hardest to do my best every single day."

In this business there is no "typical" workday, she says. "The work may be the same, but each customer is different and treated individually."

"We received our D2 visas and are officially on our way to citizenship," shares Ian, a client. *"This would have been impossible without the help and guidance of Rosário Vital! She held our hand throughout the entire process which (took) every bit of a year from start to finish. I cannot recommend her services highly enough … she has also become a friend to us in Portugal and someone we absolutely adore and love to be with."*

Regarding advice to our readers, Rosário shares these words: "Learn (about) the laws of Portugal and, when in doubt, engage an attorney to protect your rights."

Honorable Mentions
Readers recommended quite a few attorneys in Portugal practicing especially with expats, immigrants, and foreigners:

§ **Victor Queiroz** (Braga) is registered to practice law in Portugal and Brazil. "I live in Portugal, the country I love the most," he says. In 2020, Victor and his partners created VivEurope, aimed at assisting people and companies to settle in Portugal. VivEurope publishes the most extensive library of independently written articles about moving to—and living in—Portugal, often comparing it to living in other countries.

§ "My husband and I spoke with about a dozen lawyers to get help with our accounting and the D7 visa," shares Michelle. "Of those dozen, I'd say about half either never responded, some ghosted us completely even after paying for an initial consultation by Zoom, and maybe a handful seemed to actually know what to do and, of them, only one or two knew enough about the NHR tax regime to be able to help us with a complicated financial situation. **Jorge Ferraz** (F+AS, Lisbon & Porto) seemed friendly enough but very aggressive and fairly informed and seemed able to help."

§ "I have been working with **Andreia Gaspar Pires** for the last two years, offers Noelia. "Her office is located in the Jardim, in front of the Câmara of Penamacor. Very efficient, trustworthy and follows the law by the book. She always answers phone calls, emails, and WhatsApp straight away or as soon as she is available. She can sign buy and sell property contracts, power of attorney, matriculation of cars, and many other cases."

§ "We are accountants and work closely with Ricardo Antunes (Coimbra)," adds Carol. "He is very good."

§ "We used **Sara Sousa Rebolo** of Caiado Guerreiro (Lisbon, Porto & Faro)," states Djuna. "Good English. Gay/lesbian friendly. Very professional."

§ "**Bruno Dias** (Lisbon) from Berna Advogados has been our lawyer for decades now," cheers client José Pinto. "We recommend unreservedly."

§ "We are using **Vasco Seabra Barreira** of Cruz, Oliveria & Asociados in Lisbon," states Paul. "He has been wonderful. My husband received his CRUE and now (Vasco) is working on my family reunification visa. We are in Saldanha, Lisbon."

§ "I've had great experiences working with Martinez Chevarria, with offices in Estoril and Lisboa," offers Aurelien.

§ Braddlee says, "We've been quite happy with GFDL—**Gil Figueira & Devillet Lima Advogados** in Lisbon. Very supportive of us as a same-sex married couple, capable and professional, good communication, and also familiar with US law and taxation. They handled our visa and residency, NHR, customs clearance for bringing over our car and belongings, review of leases, conversion of US driver licenses to Portugal, the CPCV, our property purchase, mortgage, architect and construction contracts, filing for tax incentives related to our renovation, our Portuguese income tax filings, our new Portuguese wills and advance directives, and have assisted in clearing some disputes with neighbors in an adjoining building related to our renovation. They have typically charged on a price by project basis, and only occasionally on an hourly rate. They've never run the clock on us, and I've never felt a bill was excessive for the value received."

§ "I use HK Consulting, an accounting company who are an English and Portuguese speaking team. Andrew is the owner. I've used them for seven years now and do everything by phone and email," Micky informs us from the Elvas area.

Bruce Joffe is publisher and creative director of *Portugal Living Magazine*.

A Belgian Restores A Lisbon Apartment

This spread is from Wily Losinos, a Belgian who lives in—and is restoring and renovating—a property in Lisbon. The pictures are amazing, with the murals that have been hiding for who-knows-how-long.

"I recently posted a before and after picture of our apartment we rent out in Lisbon. I did not expect such enthusiasm!

"We think it's from 1820, as there are tiles with that date on them. I found these detailed pictures when we discovered the murals while burning off the paint.

"We painted the doors dark green, as that was their original color (not white). Plinths in bordeaux. 1970 door handles were replaced with enamel ones from the 1800s. We kept the paintings on the windows of the surrounding rooms. The table and chairs, most likely, are from DeCoen, a Belgian manufacturer renowned in 1920s-1940s. The couch, chandelier, and golden side table are from the tenants who lived there since the late 1800s."

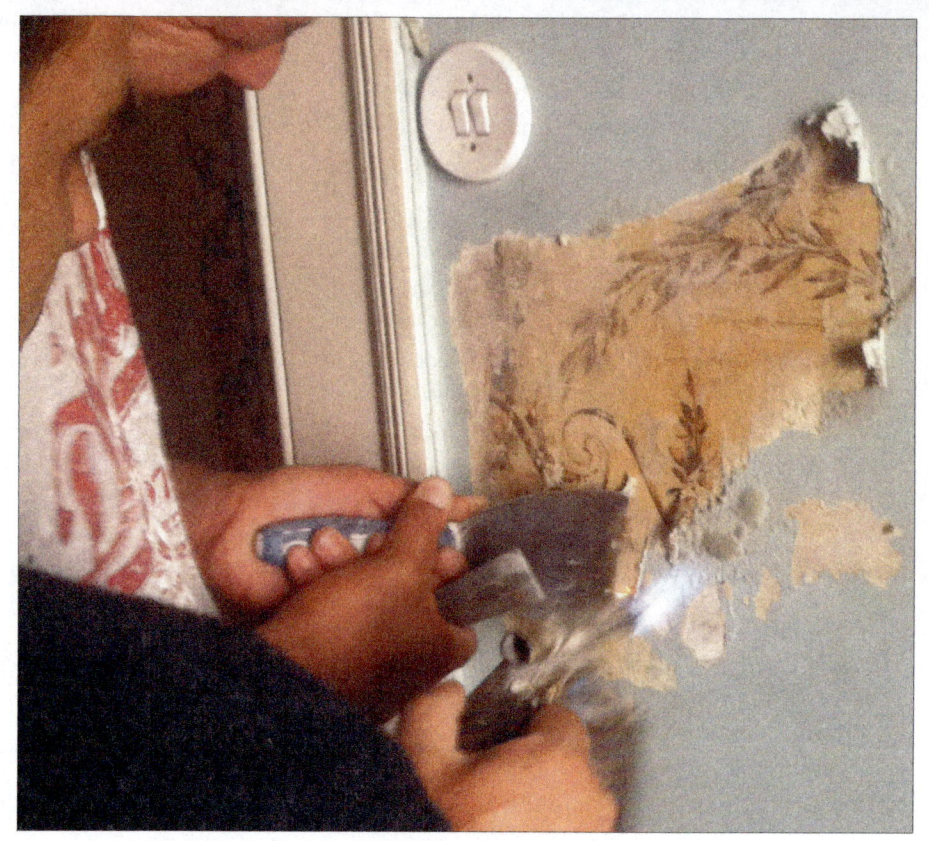

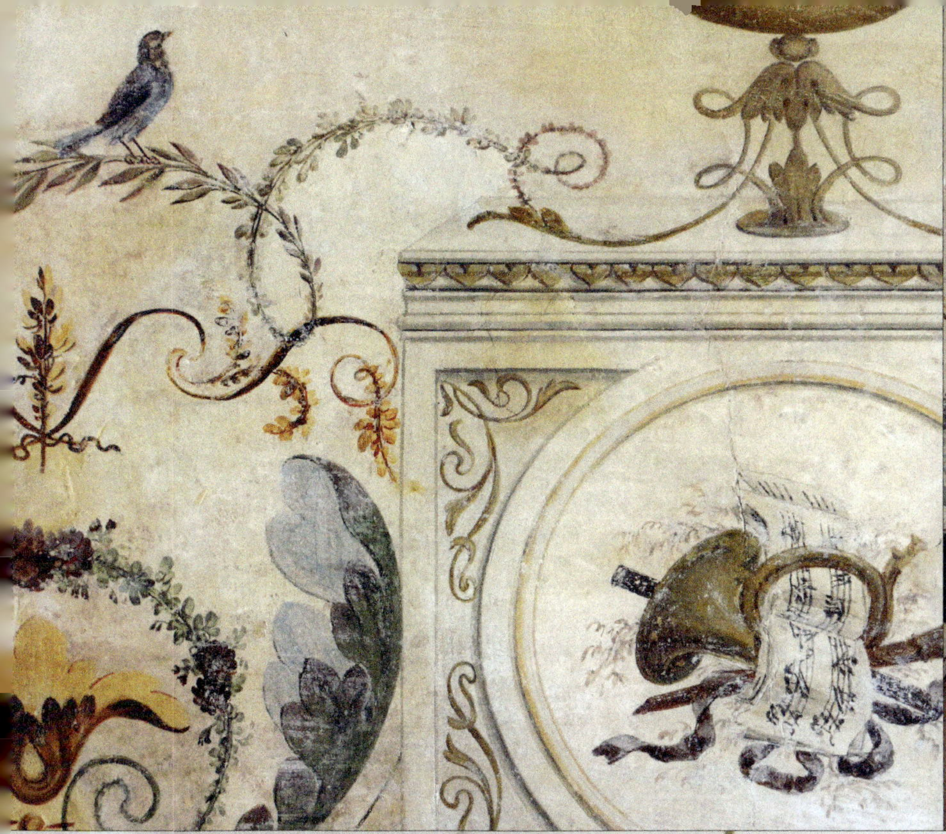

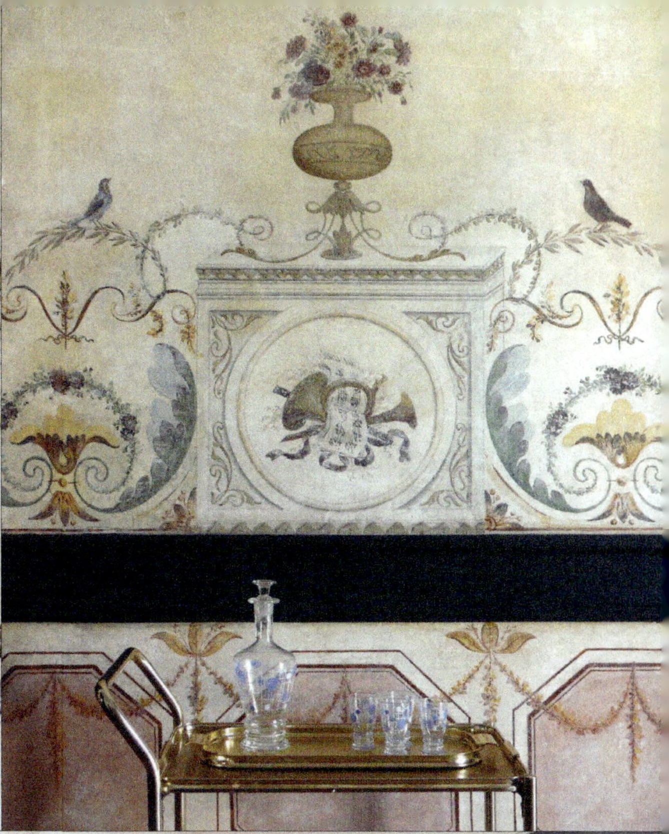

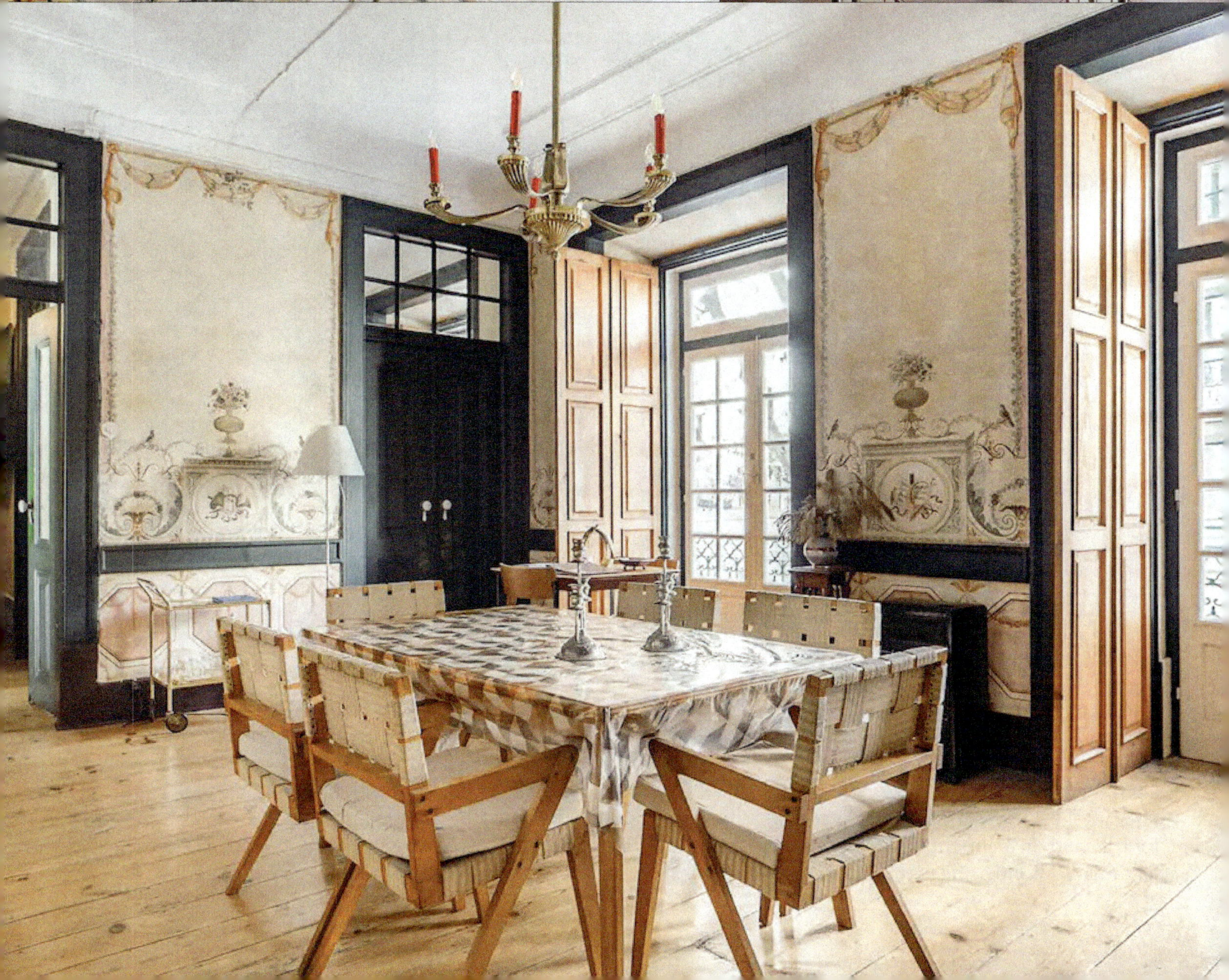

Portugal's Starring Roles

10 Must-See Films and TV Shows that Showcase this Captivating Country

By James F. Hickey

As a long-time resident of New York City, I never lost the excitement of seeing my hometown on film. The city's iconic skyline and bustling streets served as the backdrop for countless movies and TV shows, from blockbuster movies to indie productions.

So, when I moved to Portugal in 2021, I began searching for cinematic representations of my new home. I wasn't surprised to discover that Portugal's dazzling landscapes, rich history, vibrant culture, and friendly people have made it a favorite destination for filmmakers. From a Spy Thriller to an Academy Award-nominated animated short, here's a roundup of my favorite movies and TV shows that put Portugal in the spotlight.

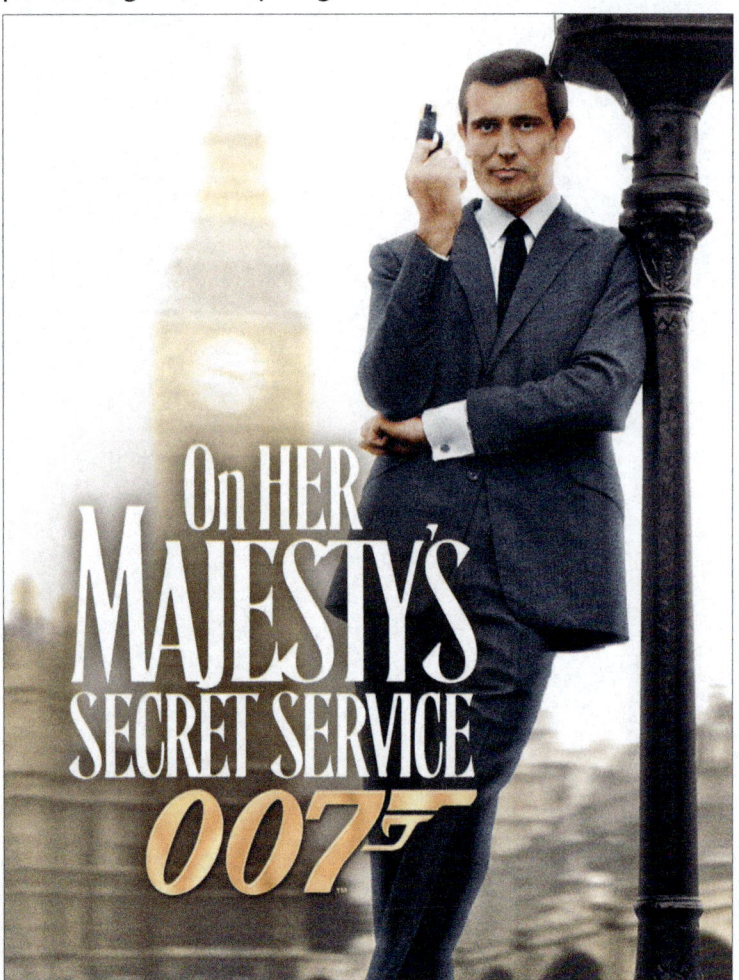

On Her Majesty's Secret Service (1969)
The Hotel Palácio Estoril in Cascais served as the location for this sixth installment of the James Bond franchise. The film follows Bond as he infiltrates a sinister organization, all while falling in love with the enigmatic Tracy di Vicenzo. With breathtaking cinematography capturing Portugal's gorgeous coastline and mountain ranges, *On Her Majesty's Secret Service* adds a dazzling visual layer to the iconic spy franchise. Despite being one of the more overlooked entries in the Bond series, this film is a stylish and action-packed thrill ride, undoubtedly elevated by its gorgeous Portuguese setting.

Lisbon Story (1994) 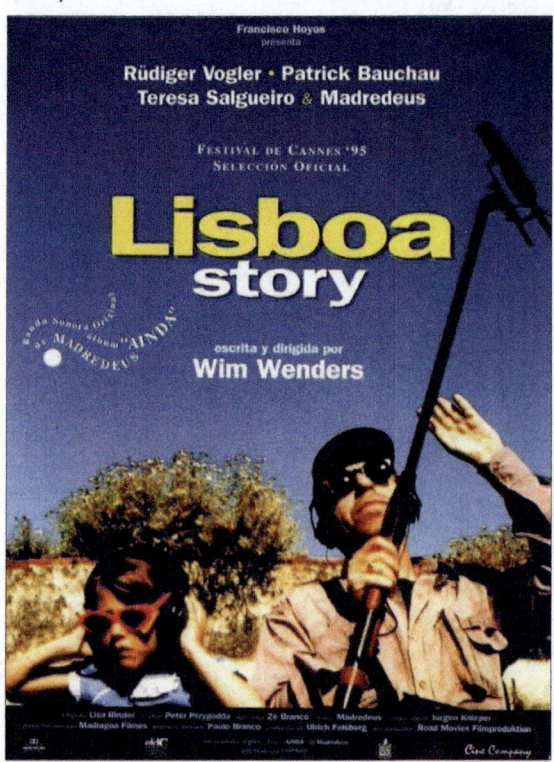
A charming and visually enchanting love letter to one of Europe's most captivating cities, this drama follows a sound engineer as he travels to Lisbon to work on a film score and becomes enamored with the city's history, architecture, and culture. The Portuguese shooting locations provide a spectacular backdrop for the film's exploration of nostalgia and artistic creativity. The imagery of Lisbon's narrow alleyways, vibrant neighborhoods, and dazzling vistas are captured beautifully on film and leave audiences longing to visit the city themselves.

Casanova Variations (2014)
This film retells the story of Giacomo Casanova, portrayed by John Malkovich, as he embarks on a journey of self-discovery and redemption during his final years. The film's enchanting Portuguese locations, from Lisbon to Cascais, offer a visual feast that enhances its themes of love, regret, and the search for meaning. *Casanova Variations*

is a unique and introspective film that may not appeal to everyone. Still, it is worth a watch for fans of thought-provoking stories.

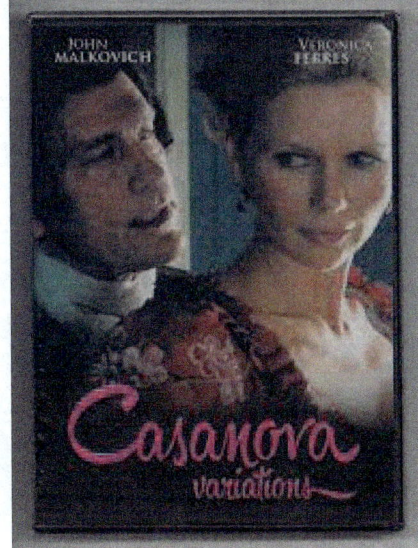

O Ornitólogo (2016)
This visually captivating and emotionally charged film is set against the lush landscapes of the Douro River region in northern Portugal. Loosely based on the life of Saint Anthony—the 13th-century Franciscan patron saint of travelers—the film follows a solitary ornithologist as he journeys into the wilderness in search of an elusive bird species but instead uncovers a series of surreal and mystical encounters. Themes of solitude, sacrifice, and the search for self are woven throughout the film, creating a powerful meditation on the human condition. The imagery is hauntingly beautiful, and the cinematography is masterful, making O Ornitólogo a must-see for arthouse cinema fans.

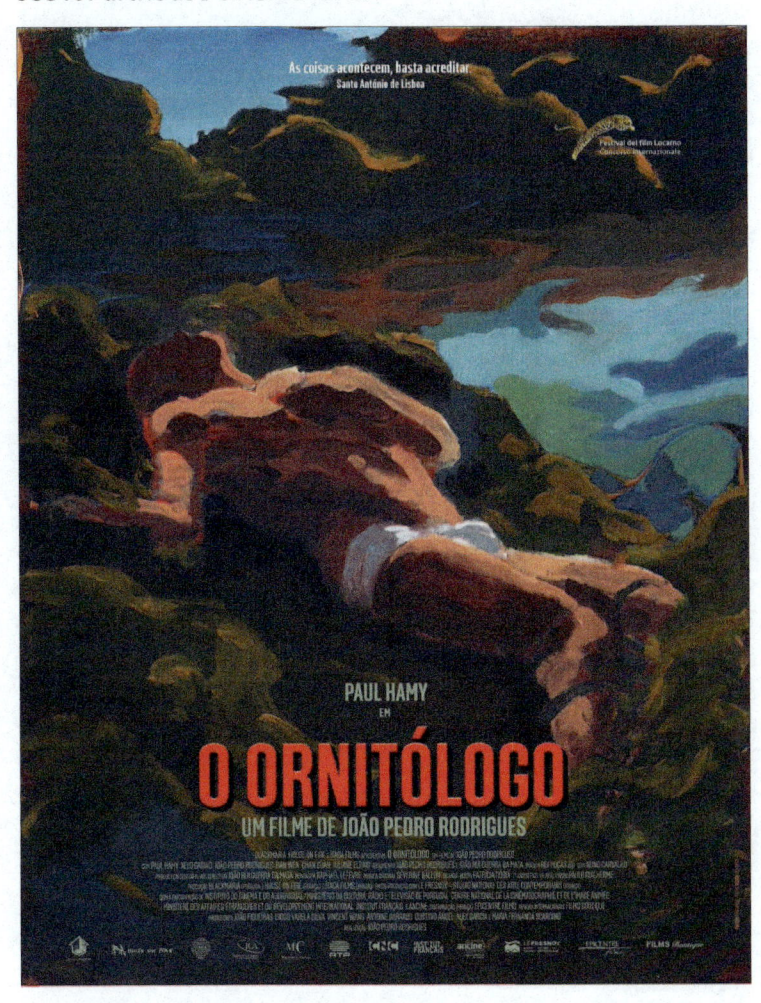

Porto (2016)
The sensational sights of Porto, including São Bento Railway Station, Café Ceuta, the iconic Dom Luis I Bridge, and other views from the Ribeira neighborhood, provide the backdrop for this expertly crafted meditation on love and human connection. The film follows Jake, an American, and Mati, a French woman, as they navigate Porto's cobbled streets and romantic alleyways while capturing the city's melancholic essence. The film is shot in a dreamlike style that emphasizes the fleeting nature of love and the beauty of this Portuguese city.

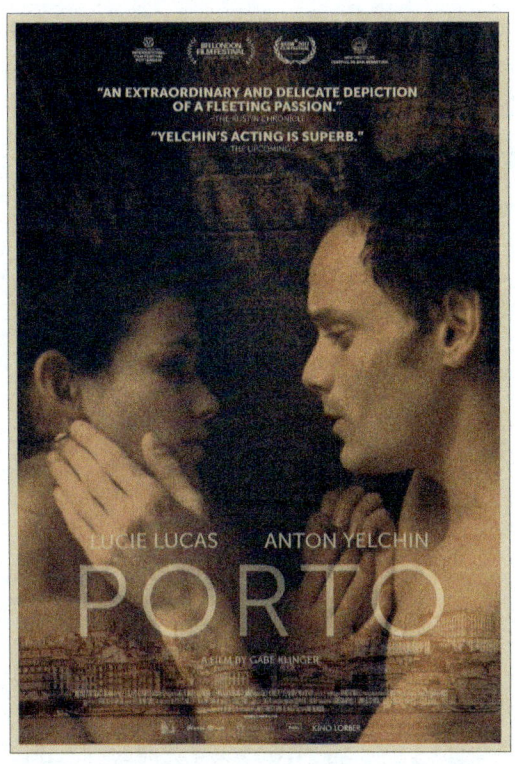

Frankie (2019)
This film is an airy, melancholic meditation on love and loss set against the gorgeous backdrop of Portugal. The film follows the story of a famous actress, Frankie (Isabelle Huppert), as she gathers her loved ones for one last family vacation before her impending death. The Portuguese locations, including the picturesque coastal towns of Sintra and Cascais, serve as a visual representation of Frankie's

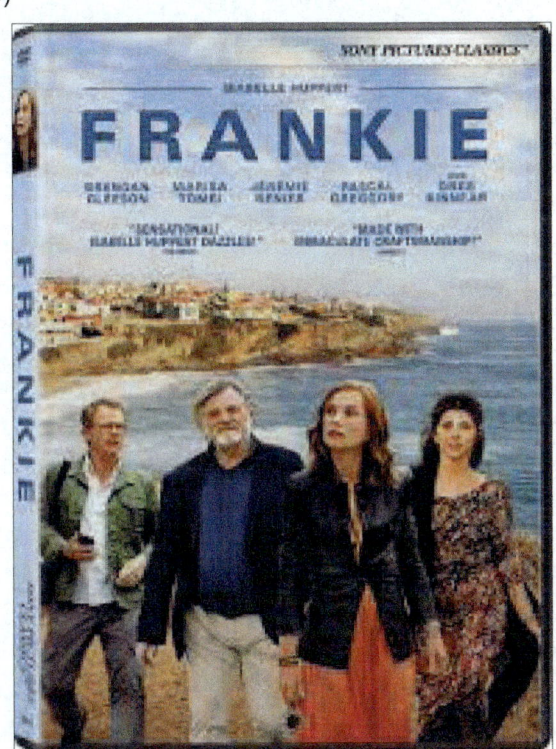

fleeting time and that of life itself. The film is a poignant reminder of the importance of cherishing the time we have with those we love, and the stunning imagery makes it a feast for the eyes as well as the soul.

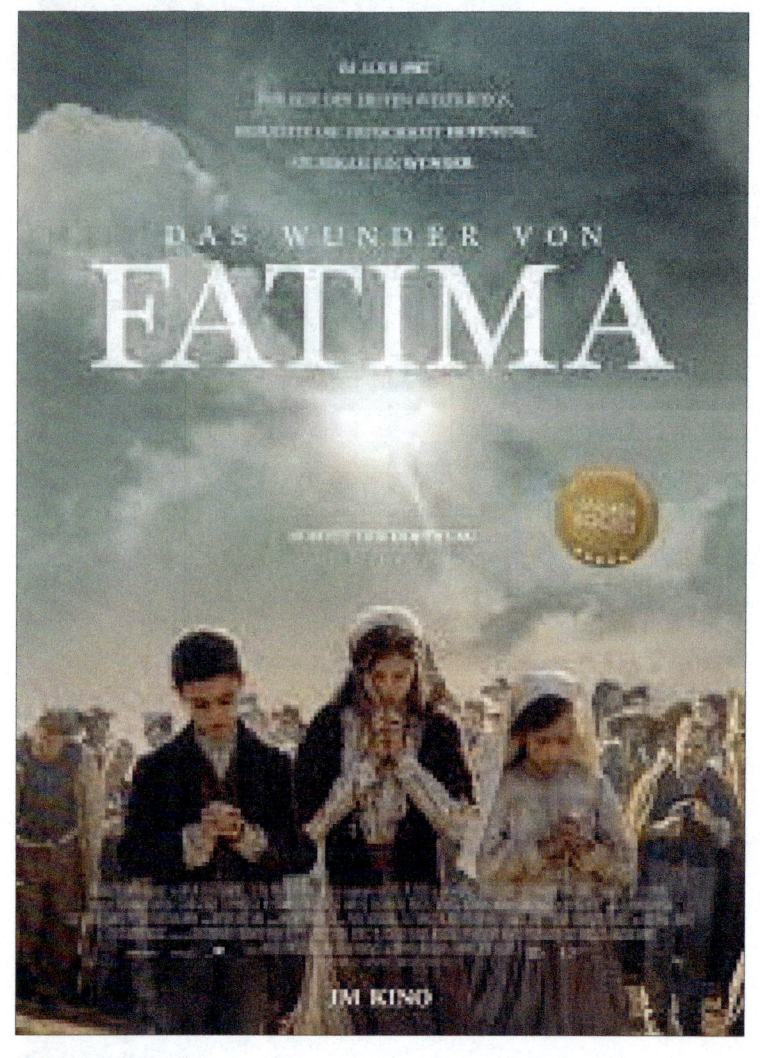

Fátima (2020)

This moving, exquisitely shot film explores themes of faith and hope. The film is a visual feast, showcasing locations in Fátima, Coimbra, Sesimbra, Tomar, Pinhel, and Lisbon. Based on actual events, the story is a powerful reminder of the strength and resilience of the human spirit. The film features excellent performances from its talented cast, particularly Joaquim de Almeida and Sônia Braga. Its emotional climax is guaranteed to leave audiences moved and inspired. Fátima is a must-see for anyone looking for an uplifting, beautifully made film with an important message.

House of the Dragon (2022)

In this prequel to *Game of Thrones,* Portugal's Monsanto and Castelo de Penha Garcia play a starring role as House Targaryen's ancestral home, Dragonstone. The show tells the story of the internal succession war within House Targaryen. The series premiere was watched by over 10 million viewers on its first day, the largest audience for any new original series in HBO history. In January 2023, the series won the Golden Globe Award for Best Television Series Drama.

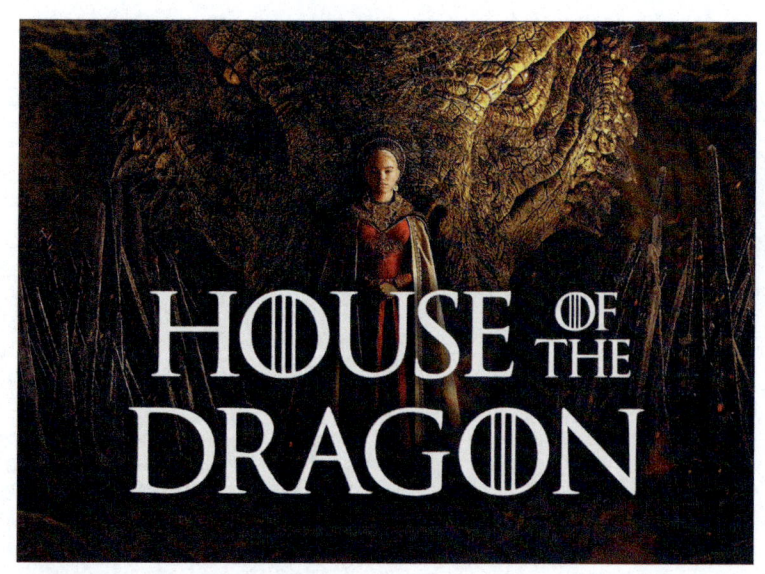

Ice Merchants (2022)

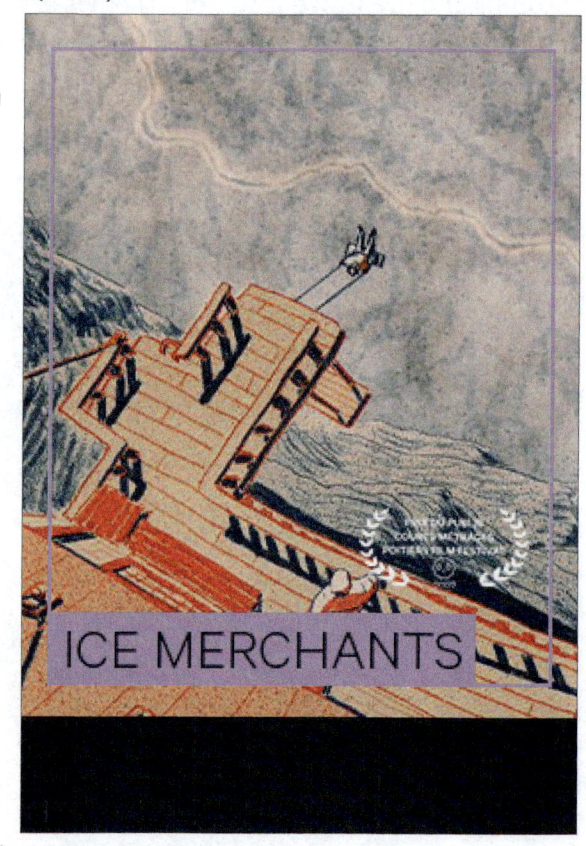

This 14-minute hand-drawn animated short film, entirely without dialogue, tells the touching story of a father and son who must parachute from their home on a cliffside to the village below, where they sell their ice. The film is the first-ever Portuguese animation to be awarded at the Cannes Film Festival and the first-ever Portuguese production to be nominated for an Academy award. Already, Ice Merchants has won an Annie Award, the "Oscar of animation," in the Best Short Film category.

João Gonzales, Director—Ice Merchants

HOW TO WATCH
For readers who want to stream or purchase the movies mentioned above, one great resource is JustWatch.com. This website is an online movie and TV show search engine that allows users to easily find where to stream their favorite movies and shows on their favorite streaming services in Portugal.

James F. Hickey has been a creative director for the websites of 20 magazines in NYC and has created advertising campaigns for hundreds of global brands. An American expat, he currently lives on a farm in Portugal with his husband and their furry family.

Portugal The Simple Life is sponsored by Leisure Launch group companies, which specialise in supporting families to transition to a simple life in Portugal.

Prefer the feel of fingers turning pages?

High-quality, low-cost, perfect bound copies of *Portugal Living Magazine* are available from Amazon.

Cost-efficient and environmentally friendly, they're great for gifts and keepsakes, friends and family, your own library or coffee table!

Simply search for "Portugal Living Magazine" under Books.

47   *Portugal Living Magazine*

15 'Cheap' Cities with Quality of Life

By Lea Melo

Living in Portugal is the dream of many people around the world. But, contrary to what you may think, it is not necessary to pay dearly to live well. Discover some of the 15 cheapest cities to live in Portugal in this article.

We did extensive research on Portuguese cities to create this list. Here, you will find cities with populations between 50,000 and 200,000 inhabitants. That is, neither too small nor too big. Furthermore, it was essential that each have its own economy and a strong local culture.

1. Castelo Branco

The city of Castelo Branco is located in central Portugal, near the Spanish border. So, it means it's halfway between Lisbon, Porto, and Madrid. Castelo Branco is a traditional and cultural place, with wholesale and retail trade as its main economic sector. For those who want to study in Portugal, Castelo Branco has a polytechnic institute.

Castelo Branco Episcopal Gardens
photo: Irina

Day-to-day life is quiet, and Castelo Branco residents benefit from little traffic. In fact, many residents only get around by bicycle. Living here, you get to enjoy many green areas and historical monuments to visit.

2. Santarém

Just an hour from Lisbon, the city of Santarém—in the Santarém district—is one of the cheapest cities to live in Portugal. It's also much calmer than the Portuguese capital, in what is called the Ribatejo region.

Santarém is a cheap option near Lisbon.

Although in the interior of Portugal, Santarém is a developed city, with good employment opportunities and excellent accessibility.

The local economy is traditionally focused on agriculture and livestock, and the Gothic monuments give the city a unique charm.

3. Viseu

Viseu, in the center of Portugal, is one of the most famous cities to live well with little money. About 130km from Porto, Viseu is another countryside town that has attracted many foreigners to restart their lives.

In addition, in the Portugal City Brand Ranking 2021, Viseu was considered the 5th best city to live in the entire country. Access to public health is great, the streets are calm and clean, and the city is also rich in history. Viseu definitely deserves the highlight it enjoys.

4. Viana do Castelo

The city of Viana do Castelo owns some of the most beautiful landscapes in Portugal and is located in the far north of the country. It is known as the Pearl of the Minho region, and still, it has one of the lowest costs of living.

In addition to the beauty of the beach, greenery, and historical monuments, residents of Viana do Castelo have good job and study offers. It is much quieter than Porto, located 70km south, but it still pleases families.

The city is subject to strong Atlantic winds, with very cold and rainy winters and average temperatures in January of 9.5°C (49.1°F). In summer, there are a few days of intense heat, and in August, the average temperature is 20.5°C (68.9°F), good enough to enjoy the beaches.

5. Figueira da Foz

Beautifying the Portuguese Silver Coast, Figueira da Foz is also one of the cheapest cities to live in Portugal. It is just 50km from Coimbra, 200km from Lisbon, and 140km from Porto. It is, therefore, a great option for those looking for an environment close to big cities, but with quiet and beautiful views.

Figueira da Foz is a city of great tradition and historical importance, being one of the main cities to visit in the Centro region. The city's extensive beaches attract people from all over the country, and the city's lifestyle mainly appeals to those looking for calm days.

6. Ponta Delgada

Have you ever thought about living on an island in the middle of the Atlantic Ocean? You'll be glad to know that Ponta Delgada, the capital of the Azores archipelago, is also one of the cheapest cities to live in Portugal. And, of course, the quality of life here hardly disappoints anyone. Welcome to the island of São Miguel!

The Portuguese archipelago of the Azores is famous for its breathtaking natural settings, and living in Ponta Delgada is an affordable dream.

Unlike most of Portugal, Ponta Delgada has a tropical climate. That means that temperatures don't change as much each season, and the weather is always pleasant.

7. Alcobaça

Located in the central-western region of Portugal, Alcobaça is a deeply cultural city and a great place to live. At only 110km from central Lisbon, Alcobaça holds some of the most important monuments to Portuguese history.

Residents of the small town benefit from a relaxed standard of living. In addition to access to culture, living in Alcobaça allows you to have contact with incredible natural environments in the surroundings—from Serra dos Candeeiros to the Atlantic Ocean.

Living here is ideal for those looking for a calm small town in central Portugal.

8. Évora

Also known as the "city museum," Évora is one of the most important cities in the [Alentejo region](). It's in a south-central location, below Lisbon and above the Algarve, surrounded by vineyards, extensive plantations, and cattle raising. The city itself is protected by centuries-old walls, and the streets are full of history.

Living in Évora is to be living inside a UNESCO World Heritage site. Its churches, Roman ruins, and university enchant any visitor. And the "capital" of Alentejo was considered the best city to live, visit, and do business in the region by the Portugal City Brand Ranking 2021.

At 140km from Lisbon, Évora is a small town, but there is no lack of essential services for its residents.

9. Póvoa de Varzim

The humble yet beautiful small town of [Póvoa de Varzim]() is also one of the cheapest cities to live in Portugal. It is located only 35km from central Porto, the capital of the northern region of the country. Besides being close to many big companies, Póvoa de Varzim has also been a renowned bathing beach for centuries.

Living in Póvoa de Varzim, you can expect a calm lifestyle, with the great advantage of being very close to a metropolis with a lot of life. The buildings are newer than in Porto, in addition to being cheaper, and there is no lack of good infrastructure. It's in the colder region of Portugal, but still a great summer destination.

10. Aveiro

[Aveiro]() is one of the most famous cities in Portugal. Also known as the "Portuguese Venice," Aveiro has channels of water that enter the city, where the traditional *Moliceiros* boats sail. It is well located in the Silver Coast, at 250km from Lisbon and 75km from Porto.

As you can imagine, life in Aveiro is usually calm and blessed with beautiful views. The city is near the beach, has a great university, good schools, and hospitals, but it still feels like a small town. However, the labor market is still lively and there are many good companies in the city.

Also, if you're a fan of mild to cold weather, Aveiro will please you.

11. Caldas da Rainha

Known to be the birthplace of many significant figures of Portuguese culture, [Caldas da Rainha]() is uniquely remarkable. Since the growth in popularity of the Silver Coast, it has also gained admiration. However, it remains one of the cheaper cities to live in Portugal. The city is located nearly an hour from Lisbon, approximately 92.6km, and twice the distance from Porto.

Here you'll find the colorful Praça da República, the only fresh fruit and vegetable market that opens daily. You can spend the perfect Sunday munching on the town's famous desserts or fresh fruits while sitting at a nearby beach.

Caldas da Rainha has a higher percentage of foreigners than other cities we've talked about above. The numbers are thanks to international students who are enrolled in universities here.

12. Portimão

[Portimão]() is at an ideal location between the Central and Western Algarve. But despite being one of the biggest cities in Southern Portugal, you'll be surprised to know that it isn't too crowded.

In the summer, thousands of tourists stay here to enjoy the attractions and beaches nearby. Here, you find a big expat community, like anywhere in the Algarve, but also a considerable number of Portuguese families.

It's rather far from Lisbon and Porto, about 281km and 554km, respectively. This is a huge plus for many who prefer living at a distance from bustling cities.

Portimão may be a city, but it's still quite small, and you can live here without a car, for example. There are malls, hospitals, and many hotels and restaurants.

If you're tired of the beaches around Praia da Rocha, Portimão also has excellent outdoor areas for exercising and enjoying the warm Algarve weather. It's also got proper public transportation, making it easier to explore the city—but at your own pace.

13. Braga
Braga feels like a delicious cup of coffee that warms your soul. It's one of the oldest cities in Portugal, with beautiful historic streets, buildings, and super-friendly locals. Braga is situated on the northeast side of Porto, almost 40 minutes away from Porto's city center.

Of all the cities listed here, Braga has the highest number of inhabitants. It's one of the most important cities in Portugal, but also quite affordable. The city has excellent housing offers; rent is cheap, so it's home to many families, university students, and pensioners.

The museums, theaters, and galleries always have a diversity of activities to keep you entertained and connected to the culture.

14. Beja
Beja is a small city considered the capital of the southern Alentejo region. It's located nearly two hours from Lisbon, with a peaceful atmosphere and mouthwatering cuisine, in a hilly area in central-southern Portugal. Beja has a unique tranquility thanks to its ancient origins and landmarks, and like all the region, strong ties to agriculture.

The town's main square, Pelourinho de Beja, is a cozy terrace where you can sip coffee and enjoy the weather. If you're up for some thrills, you can go on a hot-air balloon trip, off-roading, cycling, or kayaking!

You'll love Beja if you've lived in cold regions your entire life but also enjoy the warmth of summertime.

15. Sines
Our list of cheapest cities to live in Portugal ends with Sines, a small seaside town on the Alentejo coast. You can travel to and from Lisbon in roughly an hour and a half, with only 159km. In fact, many Lisbon residents spend their holidays here.

Fun fact: The great Portuguese explorer Vasco da Gama was born in Sines! His statue stands tall behind the castle walls where he grew up, known as Monumento do Vasco da Gama.

The city is popular for fishing and surfing on its incredible ultramarine beaches. Would you like to know the best part? The population is significantly lower than in other cities we've talked about! So, you can fully relax by the beach or go check out the annual Sines Music Festival.

Living in a small town in Portugal is a completely different experience. You get to explore the real Portugal: far from tourism and the crowds, for a much more authentic and cheaper way of life.

Lea Melo is a content writer for *Portugal Living Magazine* Sponsor Viv|Europe and an expat living in Portugal since 2017. She loves the country with all her heart and is thrilled to share her knowledge and experiences abroad with others.

Cork, Aboard and Abroad
Shared from Visit Portugal

When you toast the arrival of a new year with a bottle of sparkling wine, have you noticed that the bottle stopper is made of cork? This is just one of the many uses of this material of vegetable origin, known for its versatility and its practical application in everyday objects. Did you know that Portugal is the largest producer of cork in the world? Here we share more curious details about the 100% natural bark from the cork oak tree.

Very environment friendly. Natural and soft, keeps the cool and the warmth when it is necessary, creating a comfortable and welcoming ambiance. Cork is one of the most characteristically natural products of Portugal and is part of everyday life without us even realizing it. The stoppers of wine bottles are its best-known object, but there are many articles made of cork: fashion accessories, clothing and shoes, furniture and floor or wall coatings, among others. The recent invention of cork fabric has revolutionized this industry and highlighted its much-appreciated properties: it's resistant, versatile, recyclable, hypoallergenic, and has thermal and acoustic qualities. In addition, it has a very simple transformation process to be worked.

In addition to objects we use daily, cork is part of the history of Portugal and can be found in many monuments and points of interest:

- In **Convento de Cristo in Tomar**, a World Heritage site, the window of the Sala do Capítulo (Chapter Room) is one of the places well worth visiting for its symbolism and connection to the history of the Discoveries. Among the elements carved in stone we find cork oak trunks, recalling its use in the caravels of the Portuguese navigators.

- The monks knew quite well that cork could make the environment more comfortable. Examples of this are the **Convento dos Capuchos in Sintra**, the **Convento de Santa Cruz do Buçaco**, and the **Convento da Serra da Arrábida**, where the cells and some common areas are lined with cork.

- The **18th century nativity sets**, by sculptor **Machado de Castro**, with terracotta figures in cork scenarios are a reference in the history of Portuguese decorative arts. One of them can be seen in **Basílica da Estrela** in Lisbon.

- In **Sintra**, the **Chalet da Condessa d'Edla** was built and decorated in line with the romantic spirit of the 19th century. On the doorframes, windows and glasses, cork is one of the most striking decorative elements.

- In the **Algarve**, **São Brás de Alportel** is a location where the cork industry was very important for its development. Currently it is the centre of a Cork Route.

- The history of cork is also present in local museums, which can be ethnographic, such as the **Museum José Régio in Portalegre**, or linked to industrial archaeology, such as the **Ecomuseum of Seixal**.

Scott Gundersen

- Modern equipment such as **Planet Cork**, at the **World of Wine in Porto**, traces the history of the material and its applications in our country.

Portugal is the largest producer of cork in the world; the country is responsible for over 60% of the volume of all exports and has an area of cork oak equivalent to a quarter of that on Earth. Such a versatile and natural product, it even allows us to produce things beyond imagination.

A dress for Lady Gaga It was with Pelcor cork fabric that designer Teresa Martins worked on a complete look created just for Lady Gaga. Inspired by the award-winning singer and actress' art and by symbolist Gustav Klimt's view of the female body, Teresa Martins created a dress in gold and silver-plated cork, hand-embroidered with beads and metallic threads, recreating the characteristic textures and compositions of the remarkable artist's paintings. The dress, which symbolises the fusion between fashion and audio-visual arts, took two years to produce and was offered to Lady Gaga, who wore it at an ArtRave in Lisbon, right after her last concert in Portugal in November 2014—the creation is still featured on the multifaceted artist's social networks today.

Cork portraits After a bottle of wine is finished, cork stoppers may seem useless, but artists give them a new lease of life and use them to create impressive works. **Scott Gundersen**, an American artist from Chicago, uses cork stoppers in his work. The first face he created was that of Jeanne in 2009, with 3,842 cork stoppers; and in 2010, it was that of a friend, Grace. This gigantic work took Scott 50 hours, using 9,217 corks. Other large-scale projects followed, some requiring around 40,000 corks. This is also Scott's way of promoting the importance of recycling and sustainable art.

Cork aboard/abroad, in space The Portuguese company Corticeira Amorim is one of the main partners in the supply of **insulation solutions for NASA and the European Space Agency** (ESA). Cork has been used for decades for this purpose; there was even cork insulation on the Apollo XI voyage, the first to set foot on the moon. Amorim's various branches are present around the globe, with offices in the USA, Latin America, Eastern Europe, and Southeast Asia. Recently, they reproduced **600 square metres of the surface of Mars with the material**, a floor used in marketing actions for the whole world, starring former astronaut Scott Kelly.

Sustainable waves In another field, Hawaiian surfer Garrett McNamara, who has ridden the biggest waves in the world, has **a board made entirely of Portuguese cork**, created in the middle of the last decade. It was a joint effort in which dozens of professionals in design, research, aerodynamics, and materials development—as well as McNamara himself—collaborated in the creation of the ideal board to withstand and surf the giant waves of Nazaré.

When travelling around the country, especially in the Alentejo, look at the cork oak and notice that it is one of the most common trees in the landscape.

It's a Portugal—and a world—of cork, and we all live in it.

Visit Portugal is the official web resource for travel and tourism in Portugal.

A Master Bladesmith

Shared from Salt of Portugal

Have you ever met a bladesmith? We hadn't until we visited Paulo Tuna's atelier in Caldas da Rainha. We knocked on a large blue door and Paulo came out. He looks like a revolutionary—someone who can bend the world to his will.

Paulo trained as an artist at the local art school. For many years, he built large sculptures that questioned our notions of weight, scale, and balance. But he was always interested in knives. His grandfather gave him a pocketknife for his seventh birthday. Later, he took him to a blacksmith so that Paulo could make his first knife.

Knife drawings inspired by old art books fill the walls of the atelier.

"Drawing is easy. Forging is hard," says Paulo. He switched from sculpture to knife-making after a friend placed an order for two knives. Paulo enjoyed the production process and started learning all he could about blade smithing, working in cutlery factories for a while. In 2012, he began making knives full-time. An order of 50 knives from René Redzepi, Noma's famous chef, confirmed that he was on the right track.

"Do you want me to make a knife?" Paulo asked.

He takes a steel blade and places it inside a red-hot oven, heated to almost 1,000 degrees Celsius. The steel seems to resist at first; but, little by little, it becomes as red as planet Mars. Then the alchemy starts. Paulo brushes the anvil with a steel brush, takes the blade from the oven, and hammers it to thin the metal. Sparks fly. When the steel becomes crimson, he puts it back into the oven until it regains a fiery-red color. Paulo repeats the process, using different hammers to bend the steel to his designs. Then, he places the blade in a bed of ashes to cool it off. The next step is to sand the knife. He leaves some of the hammer marks as a record of the forging process.

Paulo likes to rescue holly or olive wood pieces destined to the fireplace and turn them into elegant knife handles. He also uses Bakelite from old domino sets. Currently, his favorite handles come from the wood of a 300-year-old tree from the Bussaco forest.

"Each one of my handmade knives is unique," says Paulo. "And it is most gratifying to know that one of the objects I crafted is being used at a family dinner, a random food meet-up amongst friends, or on top of a mountain … in an adventure somewhere! To know these items were part of incredible moments of joy, to have an object solely handmade, is like holding a moment in history! Maybe that is why handmade items fascinate us so much. Especially, when we live in such a time where everything is immediate and standardized. No character or individuality!"

He urged us to try his knives. They are well balanced, perfectly proportioned, surprisingly light, and frighteningly sharp.

Paulo Tuna makes knives that are works of art.

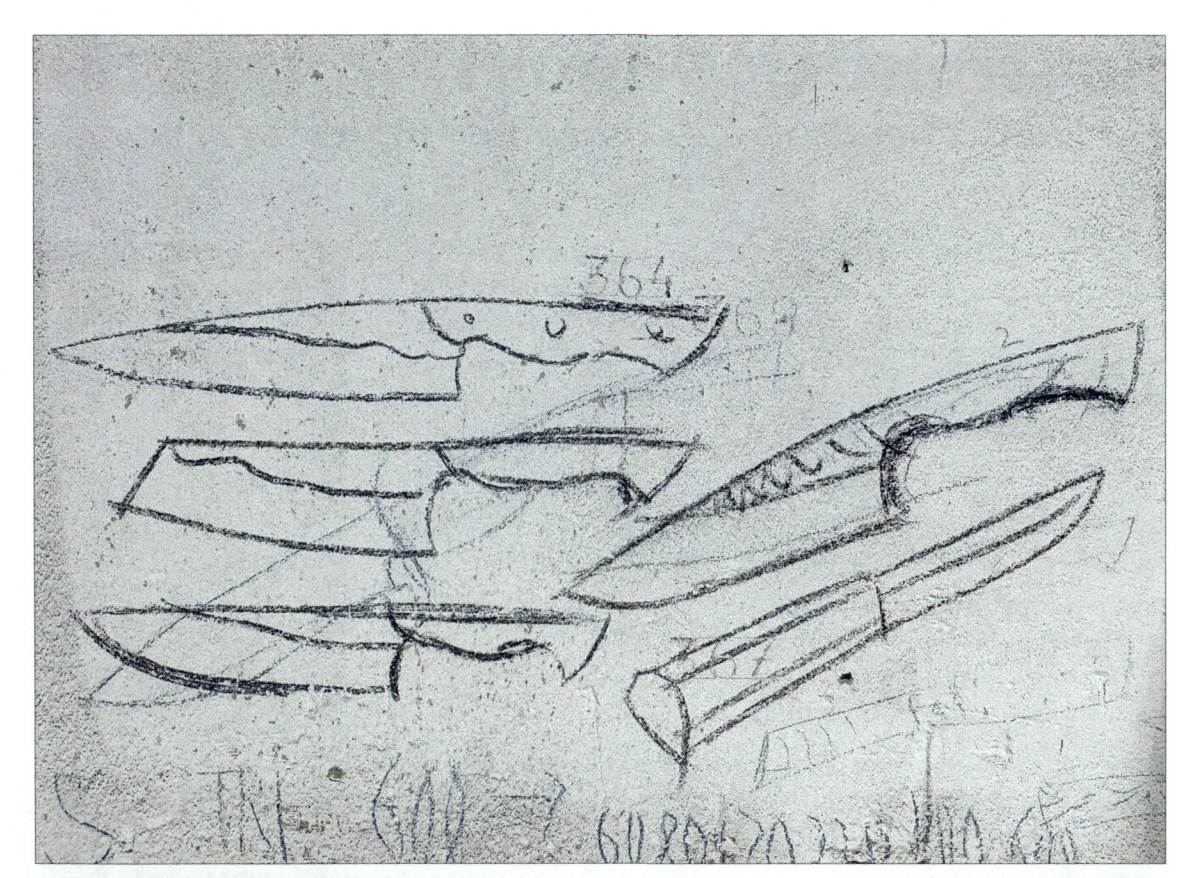

A small group of friends produces the Salt of Portugal blog. Sergio Rebelo writes the text. Maria Rebelo takes most of the photographs. Rui Barreiros Duarte makes most of the drawings. Pedro Rebelo produces the music. Pedro Teles guides their choices with his impeccable taste.

55   Portugal Living Magazine

Reverence for Books

Portugal is famous for its undying temples for reading.

By Kristin Fellows

While I was packing up my home studio in Asheville, North Carolina, in preparation for the big move to Portugal, I came across an inexpensive little bracelet I'd bought from someone on Etsy several years ago. I'd worn it for a while but then, during the distractions of the pandemic and the concerns of keeping myself afloat financially, I put it in a drawer one day and forgot about it.

It was a simple piece of metal with the words *she believed she could, so she did* held in place by a thin black leather strap.

I was writing a book when I purchased it—actually, I'm *always* writing a book—and this affirmation appealed to me. It was a reminder to keep going even as the rejection letters piled up high enough to wallpaper a room.

During the pandemic years, I was also dreaming about moving back to Europe. But where?

I briefly pondered England, where I'd spent a good portion of my childhood. I also thought about Denmark, where I have friends and family and the culture is both familiar and comforting to me. Then France, Spain, and Italy, all of which appealed to me for a variety of reasons.

In the end, it was Portugal that won out, and for many reasons—one of which is the reverence the Portuguese hold for books. Despite being a small country, Portugal is famous for its undying love for books and writers.

In fact, the oldest bookstore *in the world* is the Bertrand, which opened in 1732 in the Chiado neighborhood of Lisbon. I spent a few quiet moments there back in 2018 absorbing the atmosphere of being inside the oldest bookstore still actively selling books. While England was busy sending its poor and debt-ridden Londoners to the newly founded colony of Georgia in North America, the Portuguese were building a bookstore.

At the time of my visit, that bookstore was *286 years old*.

There's also the Livraria Santiago in Óbidos. Tucked within the walls of one of Portugal's medieval villages, the bookstore is located inside a one-hundred-year-old church. More than 30,000 books are displayed between the altar and the door.

And then, of course, there is the famous Livraria Lello in Porto. Built in 1906 in the Art Nouveau style, with its beautiful façade, spectacular staircases and ceilings, it has been called one of the world's premiere temples to reading. It's also where you know who wrote you know what.

Livraria Santiago (Obidos)

Livraria Lello (Porto)

While in Lisbon, someone suggested I visit the LX Factory, which—given the pronunciation of the letter X in Portuguese—I mistakenly thought would be a cheese factory.

Instead, I found a delightful collection of shops and eateries, including an amazing bookstore called Ler Devagar. Located inside an old Portuguese newspaper press room, there are so many books stacked from floor to ceiling they appear to be literally, or *literature-ly*, holding the building up. And who can resist a bookstore named "Reading Slowly?"

Now that I actually live in Portugal, I also plan to visit the equally irresistibly named Livraria Centésima Página in Braga—"The Bookstore of Page 100."

Portugal Living Magazine

Just one guess...which client used the services of My Portugal Docs?

Visit us online to see the full range of services provided!

NIF Application & Bank Account referral

Golden Visa, D7, Digital Nomad Visa & Others

Residency & more...

www.myportugaldocs.pt
info@myportugaldocs.pt

My Portugal Docs

These unique and imaginative bookstores give me confidence I've chosen the right country.

In the meantime, I'm still trying to finish several books of my own and get at least one of them published. Who knows, perhaps I'll publish it myself.

Because now this little bracelet reminds me not only of what I've already done, but also, what I might do next …

This is "dedicated to my friend, Candace, who loves good books," says Kristin Fellows, a documentary film consultant, strategist, and PBS station wrangler for more than 100 films on topics ranging from what American soldiers' tattoos reveal about them, to the use of American banjo music in the Czech Republic as a form of political protest; from an artist's quest to bring attention to extinct bird species through his sculptures to a white journalist examining the legacy of his slave-holding ancestors; from the story of a Christian community coming together to rebuild a Muslim mosque after it is destroyed by arson, to the story of Father Jerzy Popieluszko, a little known Polish priest who encouraged his followers to reject and fight Communism; from the life story of Wilma Mankiller, the first female chief of the Cherokee, to the story of the first Women's National Air Derby & their 1929 inspirational aerial race across America—along with scores of others.

Bertrand Bookstore (Lisbon)

57 Portugal Living Magazine

Jamming in Portugal
Relics of Taste and History of Casa da Prisca

By Margaux Cintrano

Photography by Casa da Prisca (Transcoso, Portugal)

The tradition, know-how, and reputation of Casa da Prisca's products are the result of a love of gastronomy and products from the land which has been profoundly rooted in a family since 1917.

The activities have been running continuously, and the philosophy has been passed down to the grandchildren of over four generations.

"The great grandparents made and plated sausages on sticks, where they would be slowly dried and then smoked in a part of the house where the fire and the hearth were lord and master," I learned.

The big milestone in the tradition of Casa da Prisca's products came about in 1995, when Agostinho da Fonseca dos Santos and his wife, Maria da Conceiçao Belo Plácido, decided to build new premises in Trancoso, combining the ancestral knowledge with state-of-the-art technology for creating quality products ensuring food safety. The ensuing synergies greatly increased the influence of Casa da Prisca in the marketplace, where it is now a benchmark sustainable and ecological enterprise.

The profound connection to the region where they are based has led them to contribute to developing it with the local population and resources.

The purpose of sustained and ecological development has opened up horizons and expansion of the company's activities—including the creation of marmalades, patés, and regional confectionery in addition to *Sardinhas Doces de Transcoso*.

Further, they have focused on tourism for tastings of their products and have formed a new company called *Sabores e Bem Receber, Lda*.

Some of Casa da Prisca's specialties include jams, curds, condiments, honey, extra virgin olive oil, preserves, oak cask aged vinegars, jellies, charcuterie, cheeses, patés, and foie gras de cánard.

I shared some of the most amazing preserves, jams, and curds I have ever tasted with the company's director of marketing and sales.

Among the most remarkable:

- carmelized onion and port wine
- pear and cardamom jam
- green tea reduction
- fig and dijon mustard
- orange and saffron jam
- blueberry with port wine
- chestnuts
- tomato jam with peppers
- strawberry jam with piri piri
- pumpkin jam with curry

The complete story—including a more detailed history, all of their products, recipes, a newsletter, and contact information—is available on Casa da Prisca's website.

Based in Madrid, journalist Margaux Cintrano is publisher of *Beyond Taste—Oltre il Gusto* magazine. She is one of *Portugal Living Magazine's* biggest fans.

59   *Portugal Living Magazine*

From Desk Job to Running a B&B in Portugal:
The Tranquil Beauty of Assumar Country House

Story and photos by Walt Bosmans

The Alto Alentejo is a remote province that occupies a huge part of the country. It runs from the Atlantic Ocean coastline to the domestic border with Spain. Fewer than a million inhabitants live in an area the size of the Netherlands. Much of this region has retained its authentic character embedded in beautiful, unspoiled natural scenery. The people are friendly, open, and helpful, and the local cuisine occupies a very special place in Portugal's culinary landscape.

For all these reasons and more, Belgians Hilde Appelmans and Walt Bosmans settled in Assumar in 2019: a small Alentejan village of 600 inhabitants located between Portalegre and Estremoz. They began working on the renovation of one of the oldest buildings in the village—an almost four-hundred-year-old mansion in which they now run their bed and breakfast: **Assumar Country House**.

For Walt, his love of the country and the Portuguese started in the early 1990s when he first came here on a holiday. He traveled the length and breadth of the country and was impressed by the diversity of landscapes and culture he encountered. Soon after, he started an import business selling Portuguese vases and ceramics in Belgium. He, then, lost his (first) wife to cancer. Returning to Portugal without her became a heavy task, but he eventually returned to the many friends and acquaintances they had made here over the years. He quit his job and started writing for a national newspaper while also broadcasting a weekly radio show.

In 2016, Walt met Hilde who also had encountered difficult times: her busy life as a bank director pushed her into a burnout. Once recovered, she decided not to return to the financial sector; she had just been offered a new job at the artist agency of a famed Flemish actress.

On their first date, Walt and Hilde discovered that they both had started writing a monologue for the stage out of their love for reading and writing. Walt wanted to share his experiences as a widower with the world (later publishing the book *Rooms filled with love*), and Hilde worked on

Assumar House Overview

a hilarious performance in which she compared the men she met during her years as a single woman, to Tupperware products: "50 shades of Tupperware."

They performed for almost two years in cultural venues and for various organizations until they decided it was enough—they wanted to turn their lives around. So, they planned an escape from the hustle and bustle of urban Belgium life to the Portugal countryside. After a long search—and many house visits in the Portuguese interior—they found the property they now own in Assumar. It took some time before the purchase was arranged. When the renovation works finally started, Covid hit and the team had to stop work frequently for safety reasons, which meant that the opening was postponed … by a year.

Before that, however, more difficulties had to be overcome.

Walt had just sold his house in Belgium. When the international moving van arrived a few months later for the trip to Assumar, the European borders had closed, and travel became impossible. The couple rushed to find a new place to stay just two days before the new owners moved into Walt's house. Fortunately, Hilde's friends offered them their recently completed apartment on the Belgian

Assumar House Guest Suite

Assumar House Guest Suite #2

Assumar House Pool and Garden

coast, where they stayed for three months before the borders reopened and they could leave for their new home and life.

"We were welcomed with open arms in the village," says Hilde. "The locals were delighted with our initiative, and immediately included us in the community. Some just came up to us in the streets to wish us the best of luck. We didn't come here to hide away on our property."

Walt adds: "The Alentejans are very open and friendly. Everything moves at a slower pace, and you sometimes have to be very patient before things get done. It's a completely different rhythm than what we were used to in Belgium. That's why we chose this region rather than the hubbub of the big cities or Algarve. When we walk into the garden here in the morning, it seems as if we're in an aviary. You hear the most unusual bird songs, and we follow with great interest the developments up in the nest of the stork couple that resides in our garden."

The birds started building their nest at the same time the house renovations began. This created a special bond between the residents and the storks, who raised their first nest of three youngsters last year. "It's so great to have them up close and watch their progress," says Walt.

But there's so much more to admire.

"When you drive around our region or go for a hike, I am always amazed by the versatility of the landscape. Every few kilometers it changes drastically: from mountains, it suddenly seems that you are somewhere on the moors, and 50 kms on, you're standing high on the castle of Marvão, from where you can see Spain," Walt continues. "So, we encourage our guests to get out and about as much as possible during their stay. We take them to a friend's farm; we go grape picking during the harvest; we organize a stargazing evening in our garden. Some call the Alentejo a backward area, but it is also an asset to anchor the authenticity of old customs and habits in a world that is changing faster and ever more relentless.

"We are happy and know that we have done our job well when guests go home saying that they have felt 'at home' with us. They write the most beautiful words of praise in our guestbook, which, to us, is confirmation that we offer more than just a good bed and a wholesome breakfast. Personal attention and making time for our guests play a major part in this. We won't go for less."

(Editor's Note: After submitting this piece, Walt and Hilde's **Assumar Country House** was honored by *boa cama/boa mesa* travel guide as among the very best in Portugal.)

Assumar Country House *offers four spacious suites in the manor house. In the garden, you can rent the 'casa do jardim,' a self-catering apartment for up to four, on a weekly basis.*

The Thing About Visitors

By LaDonna Witmer

*You drive to the airport at midnight, fizzy with anticipation.
You made a sign. You made the bed.
You turned on all the lights to welcome the ones you left behind.
Good friends.
Best.*

*You've missed them like a heartbeat.
Counted down the months-days-minutes.
You've made lists of delights they can sample.*

*But the truth is: You just want to fold them into your life like laundry.
Come with me to the grocery, the hair salon. We can pick up the post and belly rub the dog.
Let's fill our teas with ice and loiter on the terrace, gossiping about everyone we've ever known.
The light in Portugal, it's so baked-bread-looking. We'll watch it dissolve into the Atlantic
while we reminisce about the Pacific.*

Let's stay up late and get up later. Let's just be. Here. Together.

*The airplane touches down wheels. Progress comes in texts.
"We have landed."
"The passport control line is short."
"Waiting for bags."*

*You scrutinize everybody that exits. Is this them? Is that? Finally, the long-awaited faces.
Squeals and embraces. Arrival gate smiles from all around.
They're here. They're here. They're here.*

*The next day is jet lag. The day after, reality.
Because this is not their life. This is their vacation.
They love you. They love your dog.
But they raided their savings account to travel 5,687 miles.
Of course they have an agenda.
Tram 28 and Pena Palace and Ponta da Piedade and the dolphin boat.*

They have missed you, but also.
They are here to Pack! It! In!
Make! Some! Memories! go and Go and GO.

You understand.
You've been them, too, with 21 vacation days out of 365.
You once had that life that requires you to maximize.
You can't expect it to work the way it used to when you shared a street and a carpool lane.

So you seize every liminal moment. Squeeze the juice from every ticket line and ten-minute drive.
You obsess over the details of their person, their outfits, their inflections.
How much have they changed?
How much have you?

Too soon the week is up.
You sit on the suitcase so they can zip it.
One last conversation on the way to the airport.
You park and walk with them as far as the rules will let you.
You hug, and the promises fall like tears: "We'll call. We'll write. We'll see you soon."
And then their backs, even these are beloved.
A wave as they turn the corner.

The silence all the way home is desolate, but welcome.

LaDonna Witmer and her family emigrated from San Francisco, CA, to Portugal in 2021. She is a writer by trade, currently working on a memoir and a full-length collection of poetry. She writes about life in Portugal on her blog, "The Long Scrawl," at wordsbyladonna.substack.com.

Scoundrels Distillery and Gin School

Yes, It's as Cool as It Sounds!

By Bruce Joffe

Invicta Gin

"We are Australians who moved to Portugal to build Portugal's first Urban Distillery & Gin School, and our distillery is in the beautiful city of Porto," begins Travis Cunningham. "Our journey to get here included time spent living and working in Australia, Saudi Arabia, Mongolia, Iraq, Dubai, and Nigeria."

Travis and company moved here to create world class rum and to harness the availability of blackstrap molasses, new oak coopered casks, and Portuguese fortified wine casks including those to produce Tawny and Ruby, from generational port wine producers.

"The thing is that rum takes time … so while we were learning our craft, we started producing gin which resulted in our multi award-winning **Invicta** Gin collection."

In its first year of opening (2021/2022), Scoundrels Invicta Gin collection won four medals at two international competitions and was the only Portuguese distillery to be awarded a Gold Medal at the London Spirits Competition for its **International Dry Gin**.

The Invicta Gin Collection

- INVICTA GIN – INTERNATIONAL DRY - ABV 44%
- INVICTA GIN – PORTUGUESE CITRUS - ABV 42%
- INVICTA GIN – NAVY STRENGTH - ABV 57%

The Invicta Gin School

Scoundrels opened Portugal's first gin school and, yes, it is as cool as it sounds!

Ruminate—Pure Single Rum

"It's official," cheers Travis. "We can now say that we make some of the rarest and most unique rums in the world! The first release of our Ruminate cask collection started in new American oak and finished in a tawny cask."

It's a beautiful rum and without peer in Portugal or Europe: the only hand-crafted pure single rum made in Porto and finished in a Tawny cask sourced from a generational port wine family.

Every bottle is made from 100% recycled glass, and the closure is a combination of beech wood and cork. Each Ruminate cask collection release is limited in number as a single cask release only.

Fact Box

Scoundrels Distillery and Gin School

Website
www.scoundrelsdistilling.com

Social Media
#scoundrelsdistilling
#invictagin
#invictaginschool

Phone
+351-914-208-078

Address
Praça da Corujeira 158
Campanha, Porto, 4300-144, Portugal

RUMINATE

You can either buy directly from the distillery or online:

- Only x 100 bottles available of Scoundrels Cask Strength - ABV 60%
- Only x 490 bottles available of our - ABV 48.6%

"Our distillery hosts expats, locals, and tourists in a truly international space with events including international food, art exhibitions and music," adds Travis. "So, schedule a visit to Scoundrels!"

Story as shared by Travis Cunningham with *Portugal Living Magazine* Publisher and Creative Director Bruce Joffe.

Reabilitejo
Surveying | Heritage | Planning

Helping you take better-informed decisions when

**researching
buying
restoring**

older properties

Surveys & Inspections
building condition
thermal comfort
topography/land boundaries

Technical Assessments
pathologies
heritage value & significance
landscape & visual impact

Planning Advice
ensuring your aspirations are achievable in the context of legislation & regulation

Project Scoping & Critical Friend
helping you prepare for project delivery & monitoring

Additional Services
shortlisting advice
property & location visits
pre-purchase advice

reabilitejo.pt
info@reabilitejo.pt

A Walk in the Steps of Portugal's Knights Templar

An American expat discovers a rich cultural and artistic history in Tomar, Portugal—his new hometown.

By James F. Hickey

We come upon the church in darkness, our torches held high. The flames illuminate our white robes as we wait patiently for the four men who will step forward to set fire to the large cross in front of the building. I look up to see the castle illuminated on a hill to the west. The horses are agitated, skittering restlessly and kicking up gravel. I, too, am nervous but also proud to take part.

Though less than one hour long, our procession is part of a 900-year journey of the Knights Templar in Portugal.

"We're going to get dressed up as Templar knights and march in the Festa Templaria," my Portuguese husband explained. "They'll pay us in beer and bifanas," he added, knowing my stomach is more easily influenced than I am.

"I'm not Portuguese," I reminded him. "I don't think I should participate."

"You are married to a Portuguese and live in Tomar," he insisted. "You are Portuguese now."

One of the requirements for Portuguese citizenship is establishing a connection to the community. If marching in a nocturnal procession of a medieval Portuguese brotherhood didn't show community connection, then I didn't know what would.

Tomar, one of the centers of Templar culture, is home to the Convento de Cristo, the former headquarters of the Knights Templar. Now a UNESCO World Heritage Site, this imposing monastery and the connected castle sit in a dominating position on a tree-covered hill.

My husband and I gather at the castle grounds with 320 men and women under a clear night sky dotted with stars and a bright half-moon. I think I see bats circling the castle turrets. The temperature during the day reached 104 degrees (F) but is now a surprisingly pleasant 93. A cooling breeze blows across my new leggings and up inside my tunic. My cape ripples, and I can't help but feel like a superhero. The Knights Templar was an elite fighting force and semi-religious order founded in 1119 during the Crusades. Each knight took a vow of poverty and chastity and wore a white coat emblazoned with a red cross. I am neither poor nor chaste, but I never turn down the opportunity to wear a great costume.

From what I can tell, all the participants are local, or at least they speak Portuguese. My grasp of the language is still nominal, enough to order at a restaurant or buy groceries, but not enough to participate in the playful *cerveja*-inspired banter of the hundreds of men surrounding me. Their ages range from just out of school to grandfatherly. At almost 50, I feel reassured that if the older men are confidently play-acting as knights, I can too.

We are placed in regiments based on the neighborhood we call home. Indecipherable instructions fly at me from all sides, and I somehow end up on the front line of my regiment. Several women dressed as serving wenches and carrying small amphorae step in front of me. The amphorae are empty of wine, but water will be handed out later mid-route.

O Fortuna
Velut luna
Statu variabilis

The opening strains of *O Fortuna,* from Carl Orff's 1935 medieval-inspired cantata *Carmina Burana,* swell from speakers hung strategically along the route. The men entrusted with swords—I'm not one of those—slide them into scabbards as other men raise flags, standards, spears, and torches, and we proceed down the wooded hill toward the center of the old town.

Thousands of people line our path, their camera flashes exploding from every direction. My husband remarks that he feels like a celebrity. With so much picture-taking going on, I expect cheering or smiling faces—but I find none. People look on with blank faces, no talking, and maybe a touch of fear.

"Yes," my husband will explain later. "We take it very seriously. We're proud of our Templar culture, and we're very proud that the castle has never been conquered."

I feel the heat from the torches as I struggle to keep a straight line with the two older men to my left and the young man to my right. The teenager is captivated by his flame, playing with his torch and trying to get it to burn brighter. It pulls his attention from his fellow men in line and causes him to get ahead or fall behind constantly.

Our route takes us through winding, narrow streets. We march past the medieval-themed Taverna Antiqua in the Praça da República, over the Ponte Velha that crosses the Rio Nabão, and past the Cemitério de Tomar, where we buried my husband's father just one year ago. His death, and the resulting inheritance of his house, farm, and vineyard, are why we moved from Luxembourg to Tomar. Tomar is the village where my husband grew up. He was born in the house where we now live.

We arrive at the 12th-century Santa Maria Dos Olivais church, whose Portuguese Gothic arches bore witness to the initiation ceremonies and burials of the Knights Templar hundreds of years ago. The men, horses, and women gather together in the open square, surrounded by a greater crowd than the one we experienced along the route.

We take a knee as a bell is rung, and a priest from the church steps into the center to speak of the legend of the Templars. He tells us how they helped the poor and defended the people from attacks and how the Templar's strong faith calmed the spirits of the people. With strong emotion in his voice, the priest thanks the participants and the spectators for remembering the Templars and keeping their spirits alive.

The lights are dimmed, and the Order of Templar's proud symbol—the Cross of Christ—is lit, illuminating the matching red templar crosses embroidered onto our uniforms and shining on the pride-filled faces of the gathered crowd. My husband, a fellow knight in formation behind me, reaches out to hold my hand. I watch the cross burn in silence, and my heart swells with pride for my new hometown.

If You Go

What to See: Start at the Convento de Cristo to view the majestic Janela do Capítulo (Chapter Window), a masterpiece of late-Gothic Manueline architecture. Its awe-inspiring design includes various motifs from scripture, including the Tree of Life, intertwined with nautical references to Portugal's maritime dominance. Take a stroll through the Sete Montes Woods, visit the shops and restaurants around the Praça da República, walk through Mouchão Park to see the landmark wooden water wheel, and finish up at the Church of Santa Maria dos Olivais.

Where to stay: Located on the River Nabão, the contemporary Thomar Boutique Hotel is a 15-minute walk from the Convento de Cristo and 10 minutes on foot from the railway station.

Where to eat: Continue your journey into history by having lunch or dinner at the appropriately themed Taverna Antiqua. Located in the Praça da República, this popular restaurant offers a delicious medieval meal served on handmade dishes by friendly, costumed staff in an authentic candlelit stone tavern.

When to visit: There are visit-worthy activities in Tomar from Spring to Fall, but for something extra special, consider coming for the Festa dos Tabuleiros. Hundreds of young girls march through the village every four years carrying trays of bread and flowers on their heads. Each headdress must be as tall as the girl who carries it. It's an unforgettable celebration; the next one will occur in July 2023. Book your hotel early because they sell out months in advance.

Getting here: Tomar is an hour and a half drive from Lisbon or two hours from Porto. You can also get there easily by train.

Where to find more information: Check out the Visit Portugal website for more information about Tomar, Portugal and the Knights Templar.

James F Hickey is a former creative director, executive editor, and editorial director for the websites of Elle, Elle Decor, Woman's Day, Travel + Leisure, Food & Wine, and Departures magazines. He was born and raised in rural Nebraska, lived in NYC for twenty years, and now lives in Tomar, Portugal.

Conímbriga: Portugal's Largest Roman Ruins

By Susan E. Lindsey

Men on horseback are featured on one of the many stunning and well-preserved mosaics at the Casa dos Repuxos. credit: Ken Morgan

We're part of a very long chain of human existence, and every once in a while, it's good to connect with the ancient world. Remnants of societies that existed centuries or even millennia ago can be both astonishing and humbling.

Conímbriga (www.conimbriga.pt) is Portugal's most extensive Roman ruins, a vast site dating from the Roman occupation of Lusitania. But the location, on an oval-shaped plateau high above a river, had been occupied for centuries before the Romans arrived, first by the Celts, then Greeks, and then Phoenicians. In the fifth century, Germanic tribes invaded the site; the Romans abandoned it and headed to Æmenium—now Coimbra—about 12 kilometers away. However, the invaders of Conímbriga didn't stay and the site was then abandoned for eight centuries.

Local people have been aware of the ruins since at least the 16th century. In the early 1930s, archeologists and others started to excavate Conímbriga, but only a fraction of the original town has been uncovered. The original city wall encloses about 12 hectares, of which only four have been excavated.

This Roman road welcomes visitors to Conímbriga.
credit: Susan E. Lindsey

Visitors often go first to the site's museum to view an amazing array of artifacts: ancient coins, cookware and dishes, tools, weapons, architectural elements, statuary, and more. The museum is well organized and has signage in Portuguese and English.

Outside, visitors walk first to the remnants of an ancient Roman road, ruins of houses and shops, and well-preserved mosaics. The backdrop to this part of the town is a large, crumbling wall. The Romans hastily built the wall in the third century in anticipation of a raid. It is 12 or 13 feet thick and about 20 feet tall.

Around the end of the defensive wall is the other side of the city: more houses, shops, public baths, and the remains of the forum. The town had an impressive water system that included an aqueduct, storage tanks, channels and waterways, stone sinks, and private and public baths.

Conímbriga had its share of well-to-do folks. The Cantaber home was more

The Casa dos Repuxos has been covered to protect its many mosaics from the elements. The courtyard features flowerbeds and beautiful fountains.
credit: Susan E. Lindsey

The site is extensive. Wear good walking shoes and bring water.
credit: Susan E. Lindsey

69 Portugal Living Magazine

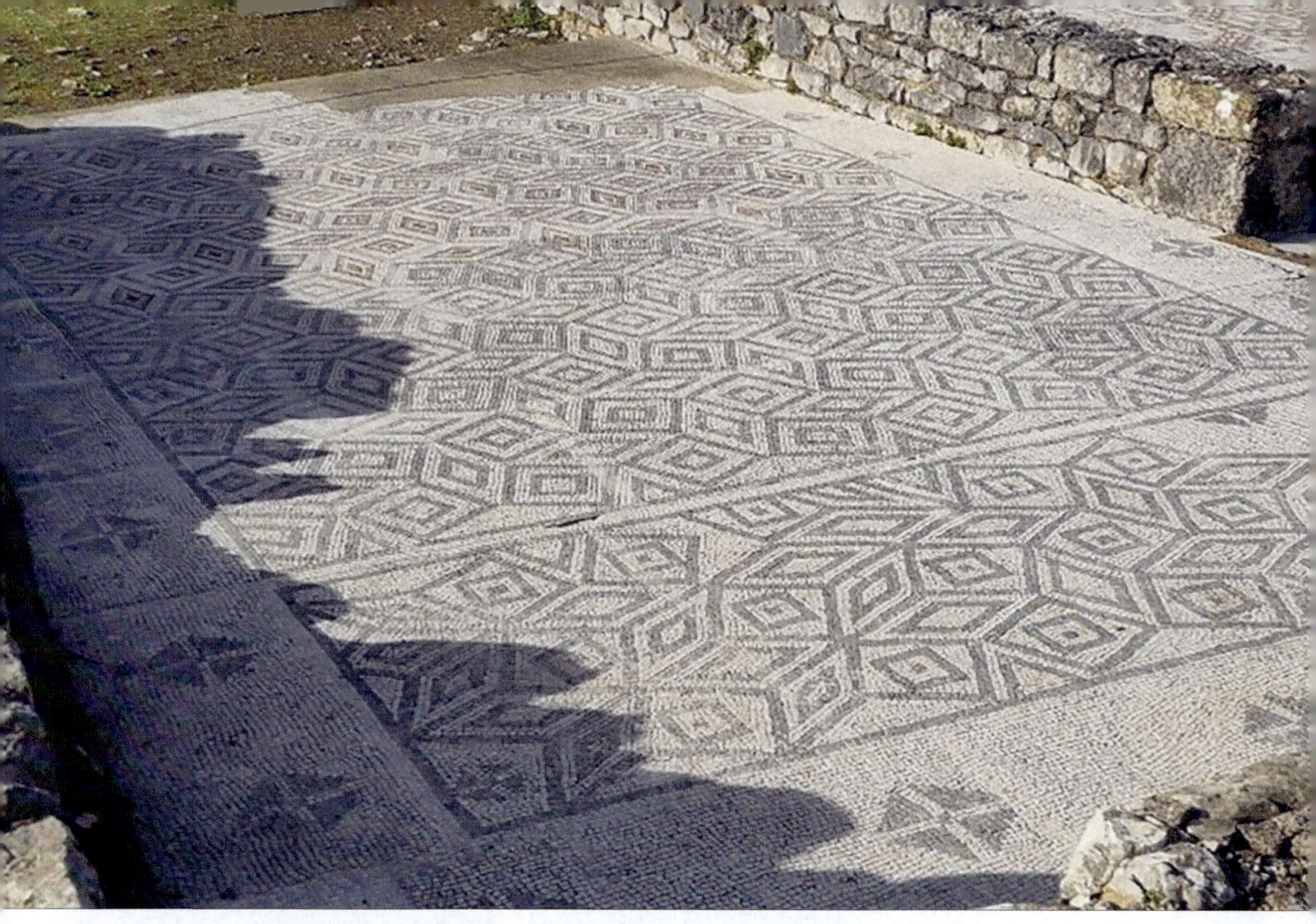

This intricate and very large mosaic has almost a 3D effect on viewers.

credit: David Stevens

than 35,000 square feet and was built around a central courtyard. A neighboring villa, Casa dos Repuxos (House of the Fountains), is not as big, but has a stunning central courtyard that includes flowerbeds and working gravity-fed fountains, all surrounded by beautiful mosaics. Many of the mosaics are very colorful, an effect achieved not by dyes, but by heating the various types of stone.

The city's gateway has deep vertical grooves carved into the walls on either side where an iron grid could be lowered into place, and several feet away, a stone threshold and anchors for hinges show where the huge wooden gates would have closed to secure the city.

Conímbriga is absolutely worth a trip, especially for history, architecture, and archeology buffs. The ruins are fascinating and in a beautiful rural setting surrounded by eucalyptus and olive trees. It is easy to imagine lives lived to the fullest so many centuries ago.

The Cantaber residence was huge—more than 35,000 square feet—and included formal pools and gardens at the center.

credit: Susan E. Lindsey

Susan Lindsey began writing for *Portugal Living Magazine* in its very first issue. Formerly Owner/Editor at Savvy Communication, she is the author of *Liberty Brought Us Here* and coauthor of *Speed Family Heritage Recipes*. Susan now lives in the Coimbra area.

70 Portugal Living Magazine

11 Reasons Why You Shouldn't Move to Portugal

By Yvonne Landry

I have owned a house in Portugal since 2018. I spend summers here and have been thinking I'd eventually retire in Portugal. We've done a VERY bad job of keeping Portugal a secret, and it's starting to really tick off the locals. You'll see your fellow foreigners taking pics of all their luggage in the airport while loudly talking about how "cheap" it is … in front of the people they are displacing.

Sure, Portugal is great, but should you rush out and move there? Maybe not. At the least, get some perspective on the downsides. Perhaps this article will discourage some people from moving.

Here are my reasons why you should **not** move to Portugal:

1. The first and most important reason is that **they don't want you here**. I'm not joking. When I first came here, the Portuguese people were almost in awe of Americans. It was like we were all movie stars. They'd say things to me like, "Do you know Tom Cruise?" (I don't.) But anti-American sentiment is growing faster than you can say: "McDonald's has a gluten-free menu in Portugal, why can't they do that here?" I guess having to get a roommate at the age of 45 because Americans are buying up all the real estate stock is less fun than it sounds. Click on the last word for the beginning of the end. Sure, it's not terrible now. They are still largely welcoming us, but what will it be like in four years?

2. **They don't have good tacos**—anywhere. It sucks. I tried to order a chicken fajita this summer and some "Mexican arroz" (rice.) The "fajita" was a burned flour tortilla covered with smashed up avocado, some lettuce, some bad chicken pieces and a chunky white substance that I assumed was a crema of some sort. Nope. Not crema. Mayonnaise. Gross. The Mexican rice was edible but had a banana on it. A banana!! Of course, we need to embrace the new country, etc., blah, blah, blah. But sometimes you want a margarita with some chips and salsa. You ain't gettin' it. Same goes for maple syrup on your waffles. Get ready for Nutella for the rest of your life. Maybe you don't care because you are ready to become Portuguese in every way? Ok! (Yes, I'm sure that some of you will find these items somewhere, but it's a big change.) You know who has great tacos? Mexico! If you can avoid getting murdered by a big drug cartel guy, they would love to have you!

3. **Bureaucracy** is a massive problem. It's really hard to get stuff done. Not only is there bureaucracy, but there's a sense of: "We don't do things this way," that can be annoying to Americans. It's very different than our "constant-innovation that has to happen or they let us die on the side of the road" attitude. I am a little used to this because I'm from New Orleans. We have a lot of this in my hometown, too. So, like a "Hey, we've never done that before and don't want to NOW!" Here's an example: In my town, there was an empty pool. The British expats thought it'd be cool to fill it for swimming. The locals did NOT think it would be cool. They went on and on about how it was used for irrigation and was NOT a pool! (I mean,

what do I know? It looked exactly like a swimming pool! It wasn't being used …) So, the eager Brit went to a ton of trouble to get it up and running. Once up and running, it was then used by the locals and ex-pats. Victory, right? No. Then the Brit wanted to put picnic tables out there to sit. Another huge argument ensued. Votes on where to put the tables, etc. Brit put the tables out by the pool so that you weren't just sitting on the ground. Locals moved said tables out to the lot next door. So, you are back to sitting on the ground by the pool. Brit got frustrated and quit handling the pool. Flash forward to the next summer: pool stayed empty until another eager Brit decided to fill it. Locals used it.

4. It's on FIRE!! Literally. I was there this summer and, **on any given day, there might be 20 wildfires**. I'm not exaggerating. One fire started less than 1/2 mile from my village. Our house is on a river, BUT there's only one way up and down the mountain. I'm a hurricane Katrina victim, so natural disasters hit me in the squishy spots. I was terrified to get stuck in a fire. Adding to my terror was the fact that, in 2017, 66 people died in our area trying to drive away from the forest. They got stuck on the road. Portugal grows a LOT of eucalyptus. It's used for paper production. It grows quickly, hence the attraction. Know what else it does quickly? Burn. It's full of, wait for it … eucalyptus oil. That makes it highly flammable. So, fires start fast and spread fast and are SCARY. My sweet neighbors told me not to worry, that I could just jump in the river to survive. When I asked about smoke, they said it was no problem! "Just take your shirt off and cover your face to breathe." Hey, I can agree that this might keep you alive, but it doesn't sound like fun to me at all. The river is about 60 degrees. I have three kids. Sitting in a freezing river with my kids, topless, sounded horrible. So, I went to the beach. I had that option because I am American and had more money than my neighbors. I spent my summer running from constant fires. The beaches don't really burn and there was less smoke, so it worked out. But I spent a lot more money than I'd planned. It's made me think that we should live at the beach, at least until that big glacier melts and floods us all.

The point is, Portugal is NOT a climate-change friendly destination. These fires will not be going away any time soon. Maybe try Bosnia?

5. **There is no water**!!! You know how Californians are all rushing to Portugal? (Well, they are.) Part of that is because California has no water. Well, Portugal is also without a [stable water]() supply. Do you think that they want YOU using it all for your long-ass showers? Municipalities are starting to discuss limiting water to certain hours. That WILL affect you. Out of the frying pan and into the fire.

6. **They speak Portuguese**. And you don't. Sure, lots of them speak English but you will NEVER know what they are saying about you behind your back if you don't learn the language and it's HARD. It's nothing like our Anglo-Saxon language. It's like if French and Spanish had a baby that said: "Shh" or "Jzzh" all the time. When I first started visiting Portugal in 2017, I couldn't understand a word that they said. There are fewer consonants, so I couldn't tell where words started or ended. Why are you moving to a country where you don't know the language? When I first got to Portugal, I thought all my neighbors were so nice. I mean, they WERE. But what I thought was them being so sweet, I now know was them nodding their heads, smiling, and speaking to me saying things like: "Hahaha, we have NO idea what you are saying!" Or "Hey, she's American! Any idea what she's saying?" They were basically making fun of me. Now that I speak some Portuguese, they constantly correct my pronunciation. They are trying to be nice, and I get it, but it gets embarrassing and frustrating. At one point, a bunch of them got together to decide they would no longer speak any English to me so I would be forced to learn the language. (I am taking lessons.) Language is going to be an issue.

7. There are **different prices for foreigners** than for locals. In my experience, it doesn't matter if they are someone whom you consider to be a friend. There will be nothing you can do about it except to be frustrated that you are being charged more than locals. They don't care. The Portuguese people think you are rich. I mean, compared to them, you are. But does that mean that you want to pay double the price for a car, or a plumber, or a nanny? This has happened

72   Portugal Living Magazine

to me more times than I can count, where I feel like something isn't right in the pricing. I'll give a couple of the most egregious examples:

- A few summers ago, I asked a lady whom I knew from my town to babysit my children. She wanted to charge me 20 euros an hour. Doesn't sound too bad, right? I'm used to paying $15/hr for my babysitter. Is that a bargain in the states? Maybe, but I only make $17/hr so it's hard to pay that. Let's do the arithmetic: at that time the minimum wage was about 600€. That's for a MONTH. It's now a bit higher; but that was the wage at the time. We can all agree that's too little, but that's what it was. The euro at that time was at $1.20. So, she was really asking me to pay her $24/hr. Then, the minimum hourly wage was 3.75€ … $4.50 in dollars. So, I was asked to pay 5.3 times the minimum wage. It's like if an American asked you to pay $38.42 an hour to babysit your kid. Did I pay her? I did! Was it "cheap?" Nope. Would she have charged a Portuguese the same price? No.

- This past summer, someone wanted to charge me €2,500 for about five hours of translation work. It was very awkward because I wasn't given a price, up-front, (despite asking repeatedly) and then I got hit with that price. They were furious at me that I couldn't pay that. I was told that I was "disrespecting them" and "refusing to pay a fair wage." In effect, they were asking me to pay 106 times the minimum wage. Can you imagine an immigrant, in the States, asking you to make some phone calls for them because their English isn't good and then asking that person to pay you $706/hour for making those phone calls?

Now, maybe you are Richie Rich and you just LOVE overpaying for your goods and services. Great! Do you also love never knowing WHAT you should pay or what the real price actually IS? This is a huge deal if you plan on doing any business in Portugal. Not knowing Portuguese, obviously, makes it even harder.

8. **No sidewalks**. Living in Portugal is much safer since you are less likely to get shot in the head at your local Kroger. However, sending your kids to walk around isn't exactly safe. Cars speed and there are typically no sidewalks or very tiny ones.

9. The Portuguese generally **treat animals differently** than we do. This is very frustrating to Americans who like puppies and kitties. There is a fair amount of animal abuse and [neglect](#). Be prepared to see that. People might leave their animals out all day, or not feed them, or keep them tightly chained without any water. Are there agencies you can call? Yes, but animal welfare is lower on the list of priorities. Portugal is a very poor country. Poverty begets other [problems](#).

10. **"They are so polite"** Know why? Because they had a dictator! The Portuguese people are well-known for being polite. This is true. They can be shy, quiet, and reserved, too. Want to know why? They had a dictator up until 1970 (look it up!) Speaking up wasn't rewarded and sometimes it landed you in their concentration camps. So, it's not necessarily that they just like you so much. They have been conditioned not to speak up or fight. They'll talk about what an idiot you are when they get home, or maybe in front of you if they know you don't speak Portuguese.

11. The **golden visa ain't what it used to be**. It used to be great but now they've taken away buying in Lisbon or Porto and on the coasts. I mean, I get it. We are all trying to escape the USA. But is it worth paying €150,000-500,000 for a house in the interior of Portugal? Not if you like to get returns on your investments, it isn't. You will also likely be in an area that puts you in the path of fire, so be ready for that. Greece has a real estate investment Golden Visa for 250,000 euros, plus baklava! Maybe consider that place?

So, there it is: My 11 reasons not to move to Portugal! The fire/water/them hating us seem like good enough reasons. I love Portugal. But I think that Americans moving there, sight unseen, and expecting everyone to speak English to them is a disaster waiting to happen. Americans moving from San Francisco because it's "just so CHEAP" is a disaster.

The red carpet is being quickly rolled up by the Portuguese people. Yes, lots of people are trying to get you to move to Portugal. Know why? Because they can SELL things associated with your move: deals on a condo in the Algarve, workshops telling you HOW to move, etc.

Know what you are getting into before you go. Visit, learn the language, and understand that you are an immigrant in their country.

Also, pack a bottle of maple syrup. And a few bottles of aspirin.

From New Orleans, Yvvone was an actor and VP of the International Association of Business Communicators (IABC). She now makes her home in Oeiras, Portugal.

Moving to PORTUGAL
Founder

FIND YOUR DREAM HOME HIRING A BUYER'S AGENT IN PORTUGAL

✓ Works For Your Best Interest
✓ Saves You Time and Effort
✓ Ethics and Expertise warranty
✓ Local knowledge
✓ Experienced market analysis
✓ Unemotional Negotiation
✓ Tackling the Paperwork

AMI 17827

info@portugal360.pt   +351 918 451 347   www.portugal360.pt

Assisted Living in Portugal:
Finding Comfort and Care in Your Later Years
By Justin Knepper

If you are planning to move permanently to Portugal, one of the things that you need to consider is how to care for yourself or your loved ones when you or they become elderly. Portugal offers a range of options for elder care that may suit your needs and preferences.

In Portugal, health care is a hallmark of the country, much like in many EU countries. The National Health Service (SNS)—the main healthcare provider in the country—is open to all legal residents and citizens. However, it can be unclear what expats and immigrants are eligible for when it comes to assisted living.

Defining Assisted Living

For the purposes of this article, assisted living can be either retirement homes or nursing homes. Retirement homes and communities offer a range of lifestyle and medical amenities specifically tailored to the needs of seniors, whereas nursing homes provide more specialized medical care as well as general living conditions. Most retirement communities are owned and run by private companies, while nursing homes can be run by either private companies or the government.

If you are an expatriate planning to live in Portugal, this article will thoroughly explain the various options available to you, which differ from those of immigrants who move here with the intent of living and working.

National Health Service (SNS)

First, let's review the basic medical resources. All legal residents and citizens of Portugal have access to the National Health Service (SNS). The SNS provides a range of medical and healthcare services, including primary care, hospital care, emergency care, and specialist care. The SNS is tax-funded, with most essential medical services available free of charge, while non-essential services and treatments are available for a small co-payment. The system is designed to ensure universal coverage and affordability for all, regardless of their social security contributions.

The SNS also provides assisted living services, including home care, day centers, and nursing homes. However, government-funded nursing homes are only available to individuals who have worked in Portugal and have paid into the social security system. This is where the difference between access is differentiated, as "expats" will not have access to government-funded nursing homes, while immigrants (who work and pay Portuguese social security taxes) do have access.

However, if an elderly individual legally living in Portugal shows extreme economic need, they may be eligible to access some government-funded nursing care and programs.

Private Healthcare

Expats looking for affordable healthcare coverage should seriously consider private health plans; not only do they ensure superior quality of care but are also extremely budget-friendly. Not only will you still have access to the SNS program, but with private healthcare, you'll be granted more choices and immediate attention for any medical services that may be needed.

Now, let's further explore the potential services and offerings that are available to you.

Day Centers

Day centers are places where the elderly can get a variety of services to help them maintain their social and family lives. The centers cater to people aged 65 and over and provide care and services suited to the needs of the user, promoting their autonomy, self-esteem, and functional independence.

The integration of elderly people in day centers also encourages interpersonal relationships, prevents loneliness and isolation, and fosters social integration. Day centers may also offer social, recreational, and cultural activities to keep the elderly active and engaged.

Typically, day centers (Centro de Día) are operated by a religious organization and may involve fees, which depend on the economic need of the individual and whether they are eligible for social security program support (if they have worked and paid taxes in Portugal.)

To search for a day center near you go to https://empresite.jornaldenegocios.pt/Actividade/CENTRO-DE-DIA/ and filter by the municipality.

Community Centers for the Elderly

Community centers for the elderly, known as Centro de Convívio, provide social, recreational, and cultural activities for elderly people residing in a given community. The centers encourage active participation of the elderly in the dynamics organized by specialized technicians, preventing loneliness and isolation, and including the elderly in local social life.

The centers also promote interpersonal relationships and favor the permanence of the elderly in their usual way of life by developing strategies for self-esteem and functional independence, personal and social.

Nursing Homes

Nursing homes, also known as residential structures, are collective accommodations for the elderly, either temporary or permanent. These structures provide permanent services suited to the needs of the elderly, encouraging active aging, and creating conditions for preserving family relationships and social integration.

Government-funded nursing homes are only available to individuals that have worked in Portugal and paid into the social security system. However, **private** nursing homes are available to anyone who can afford them. These facilities tend to be less expensive than those in the United States, but there may be waiting lists.

Private Retirement Homes and Nursing Facilities

For those expats who made their move to Portugal holding a D7 or Golden Visa, private retirement homes and nursing facilities are the only care services for which they are eligible.

Private retirement homes (or communities) in Portugal offer a range of modern care options for those who can afford them. These facilities provide a higher level of personalized care, and English-speaking caregivers and nurses may be available to cater to the needs of English-speaking expats and immigrants. Private retirement homes are often located in larger cities and populated areas like Lisbon, Porto, and the Algarve, where there is a higher demand for elder care services.

Private retirement homes in Portugal offer a range of services, including independent living, assisted living, and memory care. The facilities are designed to provide a comfortable and homely environment, with services such as housekeeping, meal preparation, and social and recreational activities. Private retirement homes can be an ideal option for those who require a higher level of care and personalized attention that may not be available in other assisted living options.

It is important to note that private retirement homes may have waitlists and specific application requirements, so it is important to contact them directly to inquire about wait times and admission procedures. Despite the potential waitlists, private retirement homes are a great option for those who are looking for specialized care and have the means to afford it.

In-Home Nursing Care

In-home nursing care is available for a fee, but usually only in bigger cities and populated areas like Lisbon, Porto, and Algarve. In-home nursing care may be in the form of visits or live-in nurses who provide care and services suited to the needs of the user, promoting their autonomy, self-esteem, and functional independence.

Volunteers

In Castelo Branco, for example, developing activities with elderly people, from 84 to 96 years old, twice a week, is a job based mainly on volunteers.

On these days, volunteers pick up the elderly clients at home, spend the afternoon doing scheduled activities (play, cognitive stimulation, and physical activity guided by a physiotherapist), have lunch, and return them to their homes.

In practice, "we help to organize their weekly medication. We go shopping with them, we take them for walks on the street, and to their appointments. We help to resolve small issues or DIY at home, as normally happens with family support, when it exists. That's why we're like family," explains Lúcia Lima, vice-president of the Associação de Apoio Voluntário ao Idoso Só (AVISO).

Choosing the Right Assisted Living Option in Portugal

Choosing the right assisted living option in Portugal for the elderly depends on a range of factors, including the level of care required, personal preferences, and affordability. It is essential to consider the following factors when making a decision:

1. Type of care needed: Different types of care are available in Portugal, including day centers, nursing homes, and in-home nursing care. It is essential to determine the type of care needed and choose an option that provides the level of care required.

2. Location: The location of the assisted living facility is critical, especially for in-home nursing care. It is important to choose a facility that is close to family members or friends who can provide support and visit regularly.

3. Affordability: The cost of assisted living in Portugal can vary, depending on the type of care needed and the location. It is important to consider the cost of care and choose an option that is affordable and within the budget.

4. Waitlists: Some assisted living facilities in Portugal may have waitlists, especially government-funded nursing homes. It is important to plan ahead and explore other options while waiting for a spot to become available.

Legal Advice and Consultation

Before signing any retirement or nursing program contract in Portugal, it is highly advised that you consult a reliable Portuguese lawyer who can review the documents and offer guidance. This should be done for all contracts signed in Portugal. As with any other country, there are some dubious establishments operating in Portugal—so be mindful and make sure to safeguard yourself and your assets.

Examples of Private Retirement Facilities in Portugal

Portugal has several private retirement communities that can fit your needs. Do a quick Google search to refine the list, and tailor it to better suit the location you are interested in relocating to. Here is just an instance of some of these homes available for consideration!

**THIS IS NOT A SPONSORED LIST.
PLEASE DO YOUR RESEARCH AND ASK YOUR EXPAT COMMUNITY FOR RECOMMENDATIONS.**

The Cork Tree Residence
www.corktreeresidences.pt

Dilectus Madeira
www.dilectusmadeira.pt

Premium Care
www.premium-care.pt

Domus Vida
www.jmellors.pt

Casa da Cidade
www.casasdacidade.pt/en

Anjos da Noite | In-Home Care
www.anjosdanoite.pt

Justin Knepper is a writer, traveler, artist, and entrepreneur. As a current Portuguese resident (originally from California), Justin has firsthand experience with making the move to another country. His passion for communication and exploration followed him to Porto, Portugal, where he currently runs a boutique digital marketing agency, writing his first novel, and working on launching a travel blog with his husband. Check it all out at https://linktr.ee/justinknepper.

Lessons Learned from 7 Weeks in Portugal's Alentejo

By Jayme Henriques Simões

They say that people in the Alentejo remember what the rest of the world has forgotten. I must admit, I have used that as a lead more than once. But after the last few weeks, I saw that it was rather true. My family and I spent seven weeks living in the Alentejo—we bought a rural farmhouse not far from Estremoz—and transplanted ourselves into an area where we knew no one.

I hadn't spent a whole month in Portugal since I was still in college, a good 30 years ago. Back then, Portugal was transforming based on its membership into the EU—it was far from any top retirement or relocation list. Over the past three decades, so much changed and, while Portugal became more modern and popular, it kept on being Portugal.

Our new farmhouse, or an old Monte, is set in an olive grove that shares the hills around Estremoz with grape fields and cork trees. The economy is diverse. Aside from olive oil are two dozen wineries, numerous marble quarries, and a blooming tourism industry. With its tall marble castle keep, Estremoz rises above the hills like a white ship and still lives mostly inside its 17th century walls. The city of about 8,000 has a thriving main square, called the Rossio, full of shops and excellent places to dine—and, on Saturdays, a big antique and food market. From there you climb to the old part of the city, set on a hill above the square. To get to the top, you cross through walls, past convents and monuments. While the city boasts an impressive mix of high end and modern restaurants, it is far from overrun with tourists. Unlike Évora, where the streets of the old city are filled with guests from around the world, Estremoz is lively but very Portuguese.

From a relocation perspective, it has the right mix; four major grocery stores, a

The Saturday market in Estremoz *photo: Russ Warren*

public health clinic, an outdoor market, public swimming pool, a highway to Lisbon, hiking trails just minutes away, and easy access to major stores in Évora on one side and Badajoz on the other. Just 30 minutes from the frontier with Spain, Estremoz seems looped into the modern world, as the border is open, and the currency the same. That means it's a fast drive to major stores, hardware, and the tastes and looks of a very different country.

Over the summer we got emails asking how we were doing with the heat and danger of fires. The Alentejo is known for long, dry summers with temps in the 90s(F) at day, and 50-60s at night. Heat is part of the summer fun and the Alentejo is much better adapted to the heat than most places. The rolling plains and hills are covered mostly by oaks and olives—with the trees having wide crowns and the space between trees considerable. The cork oaks, or *sobreiros*, thrive and, along with their cousins, the holm oak or *azinheira*, are fire- and drought-resistant. They are the basis of the *montados*, or cork forests, that preserve the environment and offer a crucial balance of nature. Our Monte sits in the middle of a centuries-old olival (olive grove) with a massive stand of *azinheira* trees. The fire resistance of the forest, and the cool night temps make the hot dry summer of the Alentejo tolerable. As does easy access to river beaches. On hot days, a nice pool or beach was not far away. We enjoyed the new *Azenhas del Rei* beach on the Guadiana, and the beach at *Monsaraz*, set between two fortified towns.

Then, people came to introduce themselves: shepherds, retired military, local business owners, and farmers. Within a few days, we had help to clean the house, cut down the overgrown fields, and haul away hay bales. A cold Sagres beer was always welcome, and we liked to chat and socialize.

We met expats, too, from New England and old England. We shared coffees and dinners. By the end of our trip, we had a list of new friends.

There were critters, too—a pair of wild foxes came by every few days. Lots and lots of wild rabbits. Local weasels and even a scorpion. I didn't know they lived in Portugal!

The house was amazing: More than 200 years of history, all with a happy vibe. Cool by day with its massive walls. We learned that our Herdade was once vast, with wine, olives, and cows. Our kitchen had been the place where breakfast was prepared, and bread was baked every morning for farm workers—a massive oven churning out fresh bread and meals. And the house had so much to discover. A Roman tomb, fruits from figs to oranges and lemons. There were olive trees dating back centuries and old azinheiras with huge canopies.

As for things to do, we were never without options. We took a tour of marble quarries, tasted wines at a nearby wineries, explored the new tile museum, hiked to castles, explored nearby towns like Elvas and Veiros. Every Saturday we went to the Estremoz market, for antiques, cool collectibles, and a massive offering of cheeses, sausages, flowers, and a few live birds. We even went to a bullfight and a running of the bulls (quite different in Portugal than Spain).

The nicest surprise was the food. Estremoz is a good-sized small city. But what amazes me is the quality of great places to eat: from high-end Alentejo cuisine to young chefs celebrating local ingredients … sushi and pizza to the classics. And even at the pricier spots, costs were well below what is average in the USA. We sampled all sorts of *migas* and grilled pork. We enjoyed elegant pizzas, carpaccio in seaweed mayo, and some great stews. Add to that affordable wines, beer, and plenty of good vibes.

After a few weeks the kids started to tire of Alentejo food. It is true that most eateries offer the same classics—grilled pork, migas, and coriander are found everywhere. The kids craved Asian and Italian food and were happy to cook their own in our newly renovated kitchen.

Food is a sort of nationalism to the Portuguese—a concept that is hard to explain. It starts with being one of the oldest nations in Europe, nearly nine centuries. It also has a lot to do with practically having the same shape since the 13th century.

I had a hard time explaining what I learned over the years—that Portugal is a survivor nation. Forged by occupation by Romans and Arabs. Born into an endless struggle with a more powerful and growing neighbor. Invaded three times by the French under Napoleon. Surviving civil war, conflict, colonialism, dictatorship, revolution, hope and disappointment, isolation and economic disaster. The world Portugal emerged into in 1143 looks nothing like the place it thrives in today. Somehow, people learned to get by, survive poverty and hardship. The food is a sense of who they are, what they identify with, and how they see the world. Simple, local, and steeped in tradition, it offers a sense of place and being. It does evolve, but it does not change much. And being proud of one's food and wine is a lot better than other forms of nationalism, making Portuguese some of the most welcoming people in Europe today.

But, behind that lacks a sense of being wrapped in a negative viewpoint and infused with hope. The Portuguese may argue and disagree on so much, but when threatened as a community, they will bond together and overcome. That's how they obtained some of the highest vaccination rates in the world. They may strive to be modern, but they are who they are.

So, after eight weeks in the Alentejo, was it worth it?

Yes, absolutely!

The people are warm and welcoming, the pace of life slower, and there is little to sacrifice. I think we were all welcomed in a strange place, and disconnected from the domestic points of worry that we left on the other side of the Atlantic.

To those who seek to live in Portugal for reasons they struggle to explain, I say this: don't run away from something, but aspire to something. As tricky as it is, learn to speak Portuguese. Read (in English) the centuries of poets, playwrights, and authors who defined our culture. Celebrate Portugal for all it is and embrace a slower, more subtle way of life.

Portugal is not perfect; but wonderful it is.

Jayme Henriques Simões is agency head of Louis Karno & Company, based in Concord, New Hampshire. With a strong connection to the Portuguese and American markets, Karno & Company speaks Portuguese and positions itself as the preferred partner and interlocutor for the growth of organizations with interests in tourism, wines and gastronomy, and export products. Jayme also administers the Portugal travel and relocation forum on Facebook.

Becoming a Better Person in Portugal

By Diana Laskaris

When my wife and I decided to move to Portugal, we knew that we would experience some big changes. Part of the excitement as well as trepidation was that we weren't exactly sure what those would be. For me, some of the changes run deep and will stay with me, hopefully, forever. It's not surprising that relocating from the United States to Portugal has had an impact on the way I live. But after two years, it has also had an impact on the way I *am*, and on who I am becoming. In some marvelous and unexpected ways, this small, beautiful, and welcoming country has taught me how to be a better person.

One of the most important things I have learned while living in Portugal is patience. The time it takes to get things done here is more than what I was used to in the United States, and it has taken some time for me to adjust. But as I have settled into my new home, I find that I am becoming more patient.

I remember the first time I took a ticket at a government office and waited for hours to be seen. I was getting restless and frustrated; but then I realized that everyone else was waiting patiently, and no one was anxious or complaining. This was a stark contrast to the "get 'er done" mentality I was used to in the United States, where every delay received a sardonic eyeroll, irritated groan, snarky comment, or worse. Discovering that Portugal moves at its own pace, which is not going to bend to my will, I found myself becoming more patient and tolerant, and it has been a welcome change.

Not only have I learned to be patient with others, I have also been learning to slow down myself. After years of constant pressure to operate at warp speed all the time, I noticed how much more the Portuguese people seem to enjoy life. They take long, leisurely lunches, and

80   Portugal Living Magazine

no one ever rushes you out of a restaurant so they can turn the table. I have made a conscious effort to slow down and appreciate simple pleasures. I now enjoy an unhurried stroll by the beach on a sunny day, a relaxed lunch with my wife and friends, or a coffee and pastry while people-watching, no rush, just savoring the moment.

Another important lesson I've learned is the power of a sense of humor. Life here can be unpredictable, and things don't always go as planned. Rather than get overtaken by stress, I have learned to take a step back and laugh instead. The Portuguese people have a great sense of humor and are not afraid to laugh at themselves. When something happens that would ordinarily make me cringe, I've learned to smile and say, like many around me, "Welcome to Portugal!" One time, when the recycling bins on our street were getting an upgrade, the worker accidentally severed the water main. Our water was out for several hours. Then, when he returned to finish the job, he severed the pipe again. Welcome to Portugal!

One of the most significant changes I have experienced is a shift in my relationship with material possessions. Before I moved to Portugal, I downsized twice, and got rid of a lot. Living here, I continue to be mindful of my space and don't want to clutter it with things I don't need. Most Portuguese don't have storage facilities or pack their garages with excess belongings. It feels liberating to free myself from constant consumerism and overflowing closets.

This has helped me to understand the value of living with less and focusing on the things that truly matter.

Living in Portugal has also helped me gain compassion, a trait I have learned by example. In the United States, I saw many people not wanting to get involved when someone needed help. In Portugal, when a young woman fell off her bicycle, everyone who saw it immediately ran up to help her. The Portuguese are not observers of life; they are participants. They have compassion for others that comes through in everyday life. I used to keep to myself, minding my own business, but now my first instinct has become to try to help out whenever I can and whenever I see my help may be needed.

Listening has also become an important part of my life since moving here. By the time I left the United States, I felt many people didn't have an interest in talking about important topics. There was no exchange, just forceful opinion taking the place of discussion. Here it seems like everyone has something valuable to say. Listening helps me gain perspective on different issues ranging from politics and economics to emotions and relationships. Even if we do not always agree at the end of the conversation, it's nice to hear what the other person has to say and maybe gain some insight from their points of view. And it's possible to do so without other people being made to feel that their thinking is ridiculous or wrong.

I've learned to appreciate human connection and a sense of community since moving to Portugal. While many Portuguese systems such as banking are technologically advanced, deliveries still require that someone be home to receive them. Socializing has become easier and more rewarding since moving here. Meeting people at events, picnics, classes, or volunteering face-to-face brings a sense of community and belonging. Living near a soccer stadium, I have learned that you don't have to be a soccer fan, or even understand the game, to get swept up in the communal sense of pride when a beloved team prevails. I feel rooted here by the interactions with those around me—whether it be talking with shop owners, chatting with neighbors while walking past them in the street, or attending local markets and events.

Moving to Portugal has brought with it many positive changes, some quite unexpected. I knew I was trading constant traffic and snowy winters for a simpler and sunnier life. And while I knew things around me would change, I didn't realize that I would change, too.

Patience and compassion are valuable traits I am gaining. I've learned to slow down, find humor in even difficult circumstances, banish clutter, and connect more to people and my community. In moving to Portugal, not only do I feel I have a better life but, surprisingly, that I am also becoming a better person.

Diana Laskaris is an award-winning author and co-founder of foodtravelist.com, a website for food and travel enthusiasts. She moved to Portugal with her wife in 2021, and shared their experiences and advice to newcomers in 101 Tips For Moving To Portugal (And Once You Arrive), an Amazon Kindle #1 Bestseller.

The Return of Roman Winemaking
And the town where it never went away

Story and photos by Alastair Leithead

The Romans were making wine in clay *amphora* pots across their Empire two thousand years ago, and in one small town in rural Portugal they've been making it the same way ever since.

Vila de Frades, or friars' town, takes its name from the monks who spent centuries producing communion wine at the nearby São Cucufate monastery which was built on the ruins of a Roman villa.

Thanks to the rising popularity of natural wines and with the help of a great story, Vila de Frades in Alentejo now finds itself at the centre of a Roman-style wine revival.

Talha wines, as they are called in Portugal, have their own official classification and the strict rule is the wine must stay in the clay pot until St. Martin's Day … on November 11th.

That's why at this time of year they are literally celebrating in the streets and singing about it in the *taberna* taverns.

Teresa Caeiro, 27, gave up a promising career in diamond mining after falling in love and doing something unusual for rural Portugal: deciding to come back home to make wine with her grandfather.

The Talha Interpretative Centre in Vila de Frades is a high-tech, beautifully laid out immersive journey into amphora winemaking.

Fifty *talha* pots are propped up under a beautiful, vaulted ceiling in her small Gerações de Talha (Generations of Talha) winery, which has stood on the main street of Vila de Frades for at least 250 years.

There are wineries scattered all around this small town and even a modern *talha* interpretive centre with interactive exhibits, snazzy videos, and a lot of information.

The family home is upstairs, where Teresa found a connection to wine as a little girl: "When I was a baby, I remember the sound of the wine filtering out of the *talha*. It's amazing—such a fantastic sound—like "ahhhhhh."

And on a recent St. Martin's Day visit, we were able to hear it for ourselves.

At 3pm sharp her husband, João, started hammering a wooden tap into a cork hole near the bottom of the clay pot while Teresa went live on Instagram to share the moment with her followers.

A few seconds later came the wonderful trickling sound of young wine draining into a bowl: the sound of autumn in Alentejo and a taste that dates back thousands of years.

Traditionally the grapes used for making talha wines are a "field blend"—a mixture of the many indigenous Portuguese grapes all grown and harvested together.

"We have more than 10 different varieties of red and white grapes such as *Alfrocheiro*, *Aragonez*, *Trincadeira*, and *Touriga* Nacional, but only my grandfather knows which is which," said Teresa.

It was historically a hedge against the weather—in different years and conditions different grapes do better, and harvest time is always when some grapes are over ripe, some are green, but most of the fruit is ripe and ready.

The grapes are pressed, and most of the fruit, skins, pips, and even some of the stems are thrown into the amphora together.

Nothing is added—natural yeasts from the grapes start the fermentation, and the solid materials form into a cap which is called "the mother."

Three times a day for the three weeks of fermentation, the cap has to be punched through with a wooden stick to prevent carbon dioxide from building up and causing the *Talha* to explode.

It's never happened to Teresa, but most *talha* wineries have floors sloping towards a hole in the middle of the room with an empty amphora underneath—just in case.

Teresa Caeiro and her grandfather, Arlindo Ruivo, with the wine he prefers.

Once fermentation ends, the mother drops to the bottom of the vessel and creates a natural filter which the wine emerges through two months later fresh, clear, and ready to drink or be transferred into something else to mature.

"We are six grandchildren. I am the only girl and I am the only one studying, so when he saw I wanted to work with wine he said 'oh my God! What are you doing with your life?' but really he loves what I am doing and just doesn't say so," Teresa explained.

She studied oenology, learned the traditional techniques from her grandfather, and now the whole family is involved in the making, the bottling, the labelling, and the selling, but what's she like to work with?

"*Muito dificil*," very difficult, laughed Arlindo Ruivo, who has made wine like this for 50 years, and his experience sometimes clashes with what his granddaughter has learned from books.

"I'm glad the young generation don't want to lose the traditional roots of the winemaking and want to take it further, and so the older generation are giving them a kick in the backside."

Teresa likes to harvest the field blend of grapes a little earlier than her grandfather, so they are more acidic, lower in alcohol, and make wines that are more attractive to younger drinkers.

He likes the more earthy, heavier wines that are more typical of *talha* and so they have two brands: *Farrapo* which is the more traditional, named after a peasant's shawl, and *NaTalha* which sells in Lisbon's natural wine bars.

They also make a special *Prof Arlindo* Red, which is the best of their best.

A dozen wineries opened their doors to visitors this year as Teresa and another new-generation winemaker, Ruben Honrado, organised the town's first festival for

São Cucufate was a Roman Villa and then monastery making communion wine for centuries and putint the "Frades" (Friars) in Vila de Frades.

83 *Portugal Living Magazine*

the increasing number of wine tourists taking a *talha* pilgrimage.

"I love the idea of natural, old wine, so we're here to drink as much as we possibly can," laughed Tina Dameron, an American now living in Portugal with her husband, Bob, who came after reading about the hastily arranged festival.

Ruben has seen an uptick in the number of visitors to the beautiful old Honrado winery and next door to his family's famous restaurant, *País das Uvas* (Grape Country), for traditional Alentejo foods like black pork cheeks and bread-based accompanying dishes.

The festival was designed to spread visitors around town, but the new festival's €45 fee for a tasting glass necklace and bottomless samples was considered a bit steep by the locals.

"It's been tough because whether we like it, we are in a small village and people are still a little bit traditional and are used to seeing *vinho de talha* as part of their culture and easy to access," said Ruben Honrado.

"But I think it's a matter of shaping minds. The money is being shared with the community and in the long run people will understand it's good for everyone: hotels are full, restaurants are full, wine cellars are full, the village is alive and it's fun. It's a win-win, win-win, win-win for everyone."

In the more traditional *adega* wineries and *tabernas*, small groups of men were spontaneously bursting into song.

We heard distant singing coming from a seemingly abandoned street and stumbled across Adega Justino Damas. Justino invited us in for snack, a chat and to hear some traditional tunes.

Cante Alentejano is the polyphonic style of Alentejo, performed by small, wine-fueled male choirs—groups of friends following the St. Martin's Day traditions.

The singing style was given Intangible Cultural Heritage status by UNESCO and the mayor of Vidiguera municipality is campaigning hard to have *talha* winemaking recognised in a similar way.

So back at the Gerações cellar, what does Tina from Florida think of the wine fresh from the *talha*?

"It's wine. It's quite good. And it works. Every time."

Ruben Honrado at Honrado's winery. Its beautiful ancient walls and floor was revealed when they did renovation and removed the plaster.

Teresa Caeiro is pictured at her Gerações de Talha winery in Vila de Frades.

Alastair Leithead: Portugal trainee. Learning how to live off the grid in rural Alentejo after nearly 20 years as a BBC foreign correspondent. Collecting stories along the way. And sharing them on his blog.

Your Last Rites
Answers to Questions about Funerals in Portugal
By Fernando Mendes

Some things are really hard to talk about—like one's dying wishes and funeral arrangements—especially for strangers in a strange land. So, we asked Fernando Mendes, whose job is to ensure that a family's wishes are honored when the time comes, to answer several specific questions. If you haven't yet discussed these matters with your loved ones, perhaps this article will serve as a good starting point.

Are there some generalities that affect the deceased in Portugal?

Burial at a local cemetery, where a grave can be purchased by the family is still quite common. Please note that, if you are not officially resident locally, the municipality has the right to deny a burial.

In fact, in big cities it's quite likely that you can't buy the grave, as cemeteries are without space and only temporary graves are available.

Regarding repatriation TO any part of the world (by road or airplane), within Europe it's common for a body to be repatriated by car (funeral hearse) because it's cheaper and less complex than by airplane. Even by road, once released by authorities, a body takes one day to arrive in the UK and two to three days to Germany, France, and Eastern Europe.

In terms of repatriation FROM any part of the world, someone who passes away elsewhere can be repatriated back to Portugal for a burial or cremation.

Cremation is the preferred choice among family when a death occurs (eight out of every 10 cases is cremated here).

Are there crematoriums throughout Portugal? Or only in the main cities?

Many crematoriums have been built in the past 20 years. A few examples of major cities with crematoriums by region:

- Northern Portugal—Porto/Braga/Viana do Castelo
- Central Portugal—Aveiro/Viseu/Coimbra/Figueira da Foz/Castelo Branco
- Silver Coast—Leiria and Entroncamento
- Alentejo—Elvas/Ferreira do Alentejo
- Lisbon—Lisbon/Loures/Vila Franca Xira/Almada/Setubal
- Algarve—Faro and Albufeira

Must funerals be rushed, as average Portuguese funerals, within 72h?

This is one of the biggest fears among expats and, without hesitation, I emphatically say "NO!" Except in very specific and rare situations where public health is at risk, a funeral is held when the family wants it.

A funeral can be held one, two, or even three weeks after the demise occurs; so, there's enough time for planning. A funeral director can guide and support you along the way.

What should I do when a loved one dies?

First, try to keep calm, knowing there are people to help you get through this difficult time: family, friends, and a good funeral director can sort out the legal and logistic details, preparing the best timing of the cremation, burial, or repatriation.

Gather all the necessary documents needed; always keep them handy.

Contact a funeral director so s/he can begin the process on your behalf.

Which documents, specifically, are needed for the funeral?

Related to the deceased person:

- Copy of passport and/or Portuguese ID
- NIF
- Portuguese address
- Martial status (single, divorced, married, widowed)
- Name of parents, so there is no doubt as to the identification of the deceased when communicated back to his/her home country
- Country and location of birth

Related to the family member or friend (in case of absence of a family member in Portugal) who is legally requesting the funeral:

- Copy of passport/Portuguese ID card
- NIF number
- Portuguese address
- Marital status (single, divorced, married, widowed)
- Name of parents (if not known it's okay, but always preferable to know at least the first and last names)
- Country and location of birth

Must I contact the embassy?

No. A death certificate will be requested by the funeral director and issued at the public registration office. Within 30 days, it will be sent to the Portuguese embassy of the deceased's home country. This ensures that any foreigner who dies in Portugal will be known back home. Families can communicate to the embassy a member of their family or friend has passed away; but that's a courtesy, not a legal obligation. If needed, the embassy will be there to help.

Where will the body be stored until the funeral?
Often, when death occurs at a hospital and the hospital doesn't have the storage capacity, it's wise for the funeral director to organize the collection of the body and be stored appropriately at the company's premises.

My family member died suddenly. There was no evidence of crime or negligence. Should I order a postmortem/autopsy to establish the cause of death?
If the deceased had a life insurance policy, you would need to provide a bona fide "cause of death" for the company to pay out the life insurance or debt on a Portuguese mortgage. All too frequently, a family assumes their loved one had no life insurance and doesn't request a cause of death certificate. Later, they discover there had been a policy in effect. By then, it's too late. If death occurs in a hospital or nursing home, the cause of death will be documented.

Even if the authorities see no need for a postmortem/autopsy, you have the right to request one if no cause of death is available. What can be demanded from the authorities is the payment of the autopsy which can be between 3,000 – 5,000€.

Does it make sense to buy a funeral plan now?
No. What makes sense is to find a good funeral director/company and keep their contact details handy. The reason is simple: today you will pay a bit over the market value for the funeral service you want.

What I recommend is what many people end up doing with me: send me an email with their desire as to what type of funeral they want. I keep it in my portfolio, along with the names and contacts (phone numbers/email) of the closest family and friends. That way, a funeral director knows whom to contact and who will be expected to contact him or her.

What other related services can a funeral director provide?
Many times, I am requested to book, or give the contact of, a local restaurant where family can gather afterwards to have a small memorial and celebration of life.

Another common service is the organization of a bus or taxi service. Why? I'll share two examples here. First, a big group of family/friends arriving on the same plane. Since it's a difficult time for everyone, it's wise to have a bus or taxi collect everyone at the airport and take them to the crematorium, hotel, or a home gathering. I organize transportation and am at the airport to ensure everyone's arrival and be accompany everyone onboard to their destination.

Whether a group of 15/20/30/50 people is going to the crematorium, it's wise to go all together in a bus than in 20 or 30 cars. Too often at the crematorium or funeral parlor, we find ourselves waiting for someone who is delayed or got lost, especially in bigger cities where traffic can be an issue.

What are the primary documents provided to the family?
- A Portuguese death certificate to deal with assets and bank accounts here in Portugal.
- An international death certificate (with English, French, and Spanish legends according to national document) to deal with assets and bank accounts in their home countries.
- In the case of ashes to be taken to another country, a crematorium declaration shows the airline that those ashes are of a deceased person and can be legally carried in one's luggage.

Must there be a "ceremony?"
No, neither religious nor formal. Many people ask that the ashes be delivered home and/or use them at a private gathering with family and friends later.

Do you recommend a closed or open coffin service?
Personally, I prefer closed coffins, as you keep the good image of the deceased person in your mind and it relieves you of that image of your beloved one in a coffin. A framed picture on top of the coffin is always easier for everyone.

Do you charge for your services?
No. I am paid directly by the funeral companies I hire. Therefore, the price includes all fees directly related to the funeral. The only fees that are paid separately are for bus or taxi service, which need to be paid directly to the transport company.

Contact Fernando Mendes personally either by phone (Whatsapp available): +351-913-287-073 or email: fernandomendes1987@gmail.com. All funeral arrangements can be done over the phone, with documents sent and signed by email. Fernando will be there during the funeral or to deliver the ashes.

Please participate in the first comprehensive "census" of expats and immigrants living in Portugal ... or who lived here and then left.

https://forms.gle/d4KZXkFgK7az7QT67

daisies photo: Jan Van Bizar

People Want to Be Known by Their Names

By Rob Vajko

We speak often in the U.S. about the American Dream. It usually means a fair wage, job security, an affordable home, and a car that runs. Not to mention health and happiness, family, and friends.

As I walk around Portugal, I notice that the Portuguese Dream is something very different.

Because we live in an apartment, my wife and I take our Miniature Schnauzer, Goji, for a walk three or four times a day. On our early morning walks, we see the street cleaners with their small carts and brooms; they are the early risers in Portugal, usually out there by 6 AM or so. They seem to disappear later in the morning, or maybe they just move to a different area where I don't go. I don't know. There are two in our neighborhood, depending on which way Goji decides to go, and both stop to "*fazer festas*" (literally "have a party") with Goji telling him how "*lindo*" (handsome) he is. They take the time to say *bom dia* and comment about the weather. We don't know their names yet, but it's an oversight I plan on correcting soon.

People want to be known by name.

My wife and I will usually stop at our local *pastelaría* for a coffee. Claudia runs it. She knows what we like, a Galao for me and an Abatanado for my wife. We don't have to ask; we just sit down, and she brings the drinks, stopping to make a fuss over the dog. But she is so much more than the one who makes good coffee. She seems to adopt all the people in the neighborhood who need mothering. We will often see her hug one of the customers, and, more than once, we have watched her hug someone crying. The *pastelaría* is open every day, and she is always there, except a couple of times a year when she travels back to Germany where she spent many years, to visit friends and family.

At our local grocery store, we see the same cashiers, day after day. In the USA, cashiers seem to be on a conveyor belt, and never the same one is seen at any store—or even check-out line—for long.

One of my favorite restaurants is owned by Marcos who lived many years in France, something that we have in common; so, we communicate in French because, well … because we can. Marcos and his wife have one week off a year and are closed on Mondays. Their restaurant serves a €6.00 "*Prato do Dia*" which includes soup, a choice of fish or meat as the main dish, a small carafe of red wine, a choice of dessert, and coffee. Because they are next to the canal and have a large billboard, they are usually packed at lunch time. I was recently talking to Marcos, and he was telling me that his landlord wants him and his family to move out because he wants to turn their apartment into an Airbnb. He's figured out that he can make a lot more money, especially in the summer, when he can charge a lot more. Marcos was complaining that there was nothing available for rent in Aveiro. He asked me where I live, and I told him. He asked me how much I was paying for our T3. I told him and he shook his head. "This is a problem," he said. "We could never afford that!"

I didn't know what to say. I felt guilty because I could.

In the apartment below us is a couple who live with their son in his late 20s. He has a job, a decent job, but he is still living at home because he cannot afford his own place. I have a friend, a very intelligent and dedicated teacher and trainer. She works with the developmentally disabled. She also teaches classes at the university. She only makes about €1,000/month.

The street sweepers of Portugal, the Claudias who run the pastelarías and paderías, the cashiers, the shop keepers, the waiters, the young men who still must live at home, the restaurant owners, and even the teachers, don't have the "American dream." They won't retire to another country when they get older. Most will never own the single, detached home with a yard and white picket fence. Most will never get a promotion to a better paying job because there aren't any managerial positions in a pastalería or in the small shop or restaurant they run.

I am not in their shoes. I am not Portuguese. As much as I would like to belong here, I never will. Most of us who have moved here to enjoy our golden years have worked long and hard and put money away. We will never completely belong. We will always be the foreigners, the immigrants.

The street sweepers, the shopkeepers, the cashiers, and the rest don't resent us being here, and I love them for it. I have never once been made to feel they begrudge us the life that we are able to live in their country. They continue to serve us lunch with a smile, they continue to ask how our day is going as they ring up our purchases, and continue to smile and greet us when we meet them in the street. They are thrilled that we love their country enough to move here.

I haven't asked them about the "Portuguese dream," but believe that it's something simpler. I suspect it involves family dinners and afternoons at the beach. It involves holding their grandkids and holding hands with their spouse, as I see so many of the older couples doing. It involves good wine and good food and *bacalhau* at Christmas.

The truth is that the American dream comes with a price.

Right now, half of all bankruptcies in America are because of medical bills. Right now, there are elderly people in America who can't afford the medication they need. There are veterans who aren't getting the help they need because of money or staff. There are half a million people who don't have a home and live on the streets. Many more are on the brink.

I don't have the answers; I wish I did. I do know, however, that for me, at least, one of the reasons my wife and I moved here was to redefine what "the dream" really is. We have private health insurance because we don't want to take advantage of a system we haven't paid into or unable to afford medicine that we might need. Beyond that, however, I think that for us, the dream has radically changed. We rent; we no longer own a home (it never did have the white picket fence). I still work part-time (40 hours a month) but no longer spend hours stuck in traffic to and from work. Life has slowed down. We take more walks. We stop for coffee daily. We meet up with friends more often and welcome many more into our home.

We've given up on the American dream and hope that what we've found is closer, at least in some ways, to the Portuguese one.

From Federal Way, Washington (USA), Rob and Jody Vajko now live in Aveiro.

The Power of Rain

A DIGGER DOYLE MYSTERY

Rosalie Rayburn

It takes courage to move to another land and build a new life. In the 1800s, more than 16,000 formerly enslaved and freeborn black people migrated from the United States to Liberia to start over.

Read the true story of sixteen of them in *Liberty Brought Us Here* by Susan E. Lindsey.

liberty brought us here

THE TRUE STORY OF AMERICAN SLAVES WHO MIGRATED TO LIBERIA

Available in print, e-book, and audio formats from University Press of Kentucky (www.KentuckyPress.com), Amazon, or Barnes & Noble.

www.SusanELindsey.com

The Myth of Becoming a Local

By Deborah Dahab

I cannot even count the number of clients who have told me that they "want to become a local." They share their desire to immerse themselves in the new country, have the same habits and customs … ultimately, they say they want to *feel* like a local.

Almost always when I hear this, I bite my tongue, or I'll tell them that's impossible. Just as a snake can't fly, a foreigner can't become a local. We can master the language, have all the costumes—but we cannot become what we are not.

When I ask clients "What does becoming a local mean to you?" the answers are always some version of to "feel a sense of belonging" and "feel like they don't stand out." Some people refer to how locals and foreigners are perceived—the latter being frowned upon. So, in the end, what they really want is to feel "normal" or "accepted."

The thing is, I believe that becoming a local not only is impossible; it is overrated. And in the next part of this article, I'll share why and an alternative … so, please, keep reading.

1. **It's really about a feeling of belonging.**
   Feeling that we belong somewhere is a lot more profound than mastering the language, knowing—and following—the norms. That's because the sense of belonging has to do with shared values. And that's what many foreigners get mixed up, only to discover that some of their personal values are *not* shared by the people in their new country. When this happens, the romanticized idea of "life abroad" can become cracked or shattered, depending on how much of our own expectations are on the line.

2. **Expectations don't match reality.**
   You probably already know that—and to those who tell me they have no expectations—well, my friends, consider this: Expecting to expect nothing is an expectation. Confused? Don't be! Let's just admit that we all have expectations, and reality usually doesn't match.

   It doesn't mean reality is worse or better—that's a judgment call that can change according to your perspective—but reality will differ from expectation.

   If not for anything else, expectation dwells in your mind while reality lives in everyday life. So, if you expect to become a local, maybe the reality of becoming a local is so different it's completely different and not aligned with how you really want to be.

3. **In the end, what is a local anyway?**
   Before I share my alternative, I'd invite you to ask yourself what *is* a local, anyway?

   There's a cognitive bias most of us have called "out-group homogeneity." In simple terms, this describes our tendency to believe that members of a group we are not part of (the outgroup) are very similar to each other. So, when we are female and say, "All men are like that," or we are Americans and state, "All Portuguese are like that," it's the bias talking.

   It's natural and normal to have this bias. However, it's important to pay attention to how it can change our perception, just like looking through glasses with a certain shade: we'll tend to see and judge everything through the prism of that lens.

My point is that when we claim, "I want to become a local," we need to define exactly what **is** a "local." Are we perceiving the host culture (the culture that receives us, foreigners and expats) identically and dismissing all the variability within this group?

We can create our own way of doing things: in a sense, our own "culture."

I have been doing this instinctively and only learned a name for it when I was preparing my dissertation for my Masters in Intercultural Psychology. It's called "cherry picking."

What I do is to pick traits, habits, and customs I like the most (i.e., most aligned with my personal values) from all the cultures I've experienced. And dismiss the habits and customs I don't like from all the places I've lived.

It created a sense of belonging because I'm aware that my behavior matches my personal values. There are some things I love about each culture I've lived in and other things I really dislike. So, when we use this strategy, we consciously take the best for us and leave what doesn't fit.

I have seen so many people try so hard to fit in and feel frustrated that it prompts ideas that this country or that isn't "for them."

Or they feel so lonely and can't put their finger on why that happens.

If this is something you are going through, request my free eBook Move Overseas with Ease, where I talk about this and more to help you adjust to life in a new country on your terms (whatever they may be). "My mission is to help anyone in a cultural transition to navigate the changes easily and smoothly," says expat coach Deborah Dahab. "To create your best life abroad."

THE PORTUGAL News

www.theportugalnews.com

Up Your Portuguese

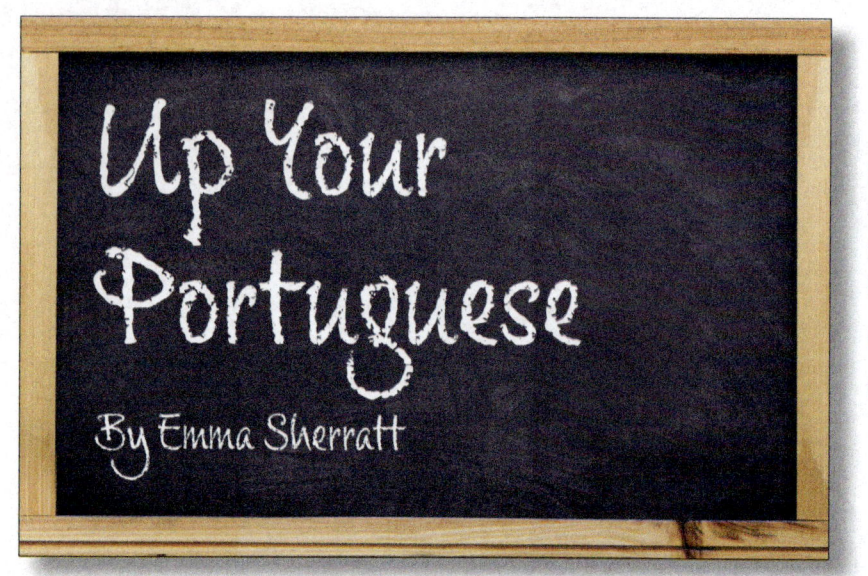

By Emma Sherratt

Here are some questions (in Portuguese!) that will make you think, keep you engaged, and, in the process, you will be coming across and hopefully learning some new words. Win- win.

Here are 10 questions. The answers are at the end.

Enjoy—**Divirtam-se**

1. **Os portugueses gostam de beber muito:**
   a) chá
   b) café
   c) leite

2. **Depois do meio-dia, ou depois de comer o almoço quando queremos dizer 'olá' a alguém, podemos dizer:**
   a) bom dia
   b) boa tarde
   c) boa noite

3. **Não lhe apetece cozinhar hoje à noite. Então, pode comer o jantar:**
   a) no cinema
   b) num restaurante
   c) na biblioteca

4. **O multibanco diz que está avariado. Então:**
   a) é possível levantar dinheiro
   b) não é possível levantar dinheiro, mas pode fazer transferências
   c) não funciona

5. **Quer enviar uma encomenda para a sua família. Vai:**
   a) aos Correios
   b) à loja de cidadão
   c) às finanças

6. **Precisa de comprar carne. Onde é que vai?**
   a) à peixaria
   b) ao talho
   c) à pastelaria

7. **Está num restaurante e quer pagar. Tem de pedir:**
   a) a fatura
   b) o recibo
   c) a conta

8. **Há um sinal informativo na autoestrada a dizer 'Com chuva, reduza a velocidade'. O que é que isso quer dizer?**
   a) Quando está a chover, não deve conduzir muito depressa
   b) Vai chover em breve
   c) Não há limite de velocidade

9. **Numa loja de roupa diz 'Saldos' na montra. Então:**
   a) há artigos com desconto na loja
   b) a loja está aberta
   c) a loja vai fechar permanentemente em breve

10. **Quer beber um café sem leite numa chavena grande, tipo 'americano'. Pode pedir:**
    a) uma meia de leite
    b) um garoto
    c) um abatanado

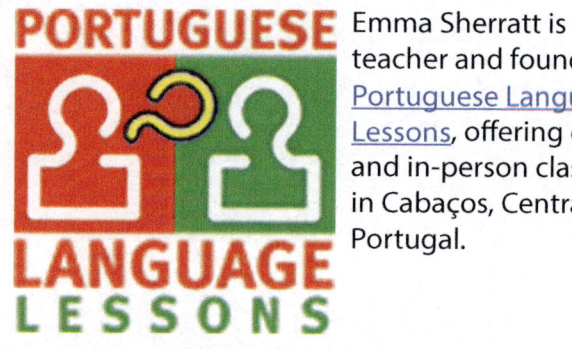

A free online dictionary I recommend is **Linguee** (you can download the app … and offline versions of the dictionary, too). **Deepl** is the translator I recommend, also free for shorter texts. Both distinguish between Brazilian and European Portuguese and offer the option to hear the words and text in European Portuguese.

Respostas:
1b, 2b, 3b, 4c, 5a, 6b, 7c, 8a, 9a, 10c

Emma Sherratt is teacher and founder of Portuguese Language Lessons, offering online and in-person classes in Cabaços, Central Portugal.

My Story: Portuguese in Six Weeks

By Amanda

Life in London was weighing me down, so in 1989, I made the bold decision to leave the 9-5 grind behind in search of a better life.

My first job in the Algarve was in a restaurant. Long hours and poor pay; but it was an adventure! Before I knew it, I fell in love with a Portuguese man named Miguel, and we moved into his parents' old, rundown house on a large plot of land.

It was so beautiful!

I also fell in love with the language and was determined to learn it. I worked very hard and became fluent in just six months!

In just a few years, our first son came along. We lived in quite an isolated area, and I had no transport. I also had to do washing by hand. A few years later, I got my bike license and bought a 50cc scooter. I managed to get a cleaning job and—finally—my residência.

A few years later, another son came along. That was when we got a washing machine.

Then at 32, I finally learned to drive! I took my driving test—all in Portuguese—and passed my first attempt. Having a means of transport was so liberating and opened better job prospects. I became an official translator in the Court in Loulé. The work was demanding and my responsibilities with the children were so great I had to give it up. Miguel did not help at all.

It was roundabout then I started teaching Portuguese to foreigners, along with casual cleaning jobs.

My relationship with Miguel was faltering; he had become cruel and often subjected me to psychological abuse. It was hard. Especially when you see no way out. I decided that I had to leave him, for my sake and the children. It took a long time, as I was tied to the house and had no real income of my own.

I finally got a three-day-a-week job paying 300€ a month! I was on my way to breaking free. But how could I? My earnings would barely cover our rent.

It was after I found myself in a dangerous situation that I knew it had to be very soon! Someone tried to stab Miguel right outside our house one evening; he was involved with some dangerous people. That was the final straw, and I knew I had to leave before things got worse.

It was easier than I thought it would be. I suggested that we rent a place in a nearby town, where the children went to school to avoid commuting, and he agreed.

I moved out and never went back. I think it took him a while to realize we had even left! Shortly after we left, a group of people went to the house and beat him up. If we had been there, we would have been beaten too.

Thank God we left!

With the 300€ a month working in a restaurant, and the 300€ per month Miguel gave me, I was just about able to make ends meet.

However, the restaurant cut my workdays to one per week and I was 200€ down per month. Desperate for money, I came up with the idea of doing an Amy Winehouse tribute act (Amy Winescouse). I found myself working multiple jobs to make ends meet. Teaching Portuguese, office work, cleaning villas, waitressing ….

It was a very tough time and, some days, I didn't even know which job I had to go to. But I persevered, and as my children grew up and left the nest, life became easier.

Today, I live in a comfortable apartment in the centre of town and teach Portuguese while pursuing my passions for music, art, and writing.

Looking back, I don't regret a single day of my journey, it made me who I am today.

Amanda was born and raised in Liverpool, UK, but has since made her home in the Algarve region of Portugal. She is a passionate teacher of the Portuguese language and has dedicated her life to sharing her knowledge and love of the language with others. When she's not teaching, you will either find her singing or painting. Visit her website.

Neighbors

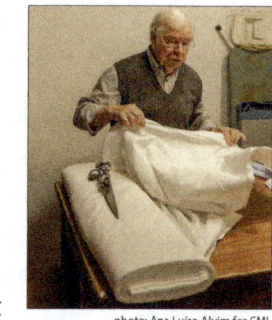

José Aguiar is 83 years old and was born in Braga. He started working at a very young age, in a shirt company, and it was this job that brought him to Lisbon, the Hospital of Shirts.

photo: Ana Luísa Alvim for CML

"I was 20 when I came to Rovil. And I have been dealing with the "health" of shirts my whole life. Never did anything else. When my second boss died, I kept this so I wouldn't close it and went to get a shirt cut in Rua da Palma.

"My wife has always helped me so much. She was the one who guided the seamstresses and taught them to work."

Previously, the company manufactured confections for baking. But each time a shirt was made, the customers "were very pleased. And one of them said, "this looks like a Shirt Hospital!" … and that's how it turned out!

"We make new custom shirts. I have shirt molds from 35 to 50. Then, when I take the measurements for the client, I see the mold and fit it to his size. On the used shirts we have new collars, fists. And we do fix or squeeze."

A life dealing with shirts leads Jose Aguiar every day to get up very early: "It makes me (feel) good to get up early. Meeting Lisbon, door to door. And I am good at talking to customers."

Portugal has some quirks. "One of the biggest head-scratchers is its love affair with bacalhau or stinky salt cod to laypeople," jokes **Ron James** who, with wife **Mary**, are frequent visitors to Portugal and publish *Wine Dine & Travel* magazine.

"Why a country known for its seamanship and rich fishing grounds would prefer salted dried cod over the tasty fresh stuff is baffling. Equally perplexing is why generations of Portuguese fishermen risked their lives in inhospitable seas just to bring back the makings for croquettes and 101 other cod dishes."

It's complicated, as Ron and Mary found out on their visit to the multi-story museum complex dedicated to bacalhau just a block from their apartment. International trade compacts, politics, geography, wars, dictatorships, and pride all played a role in making the humble cod a symbol of gastronomy, culture, and maritime history in this country!

"We didn't have high expectations for this museum, officially called the Interpretative Center of the History of Cod," shares Ron. "But we thoroughly enjoyed the museum's slick and entertaining multimedia and sensory exhibits that bring the story of cod alive. For example, in one small room, you can put on fisherman's gear and climb aboard a small dory. Suddenly, the boat begins rocking, cold air blows in, and the walls become video screens of raging waters. It's uncomfortable … but not nearly as uncomfortable as it was for the poor fisherman who has to spend 12 hours a day off the coasts of Greenland and Newfoundland in pursuit of cod. But we did get the point. It was miserable and dangerous work."

One year ago, **Reese Craighead** and I arrived in Portugal," recalls **Chuck Davies**. "We have absolutely no regrets. Of course, we miss family and friends (although we've had dozens already come to visit … with more in the coming months and year). Other than the amazing ethnic cuisines you find in the Bay Area (of California), there's not much else we miss.

"The Portuguese people have been so warm and welcoming, we've made incredible new friends, our ability to speak and understand Portuguese is coming along well, and we realize how lucky we are to have found a house that suits our needs to a T! On this tail end of our 30-day European road trip, we truly look forward to being home again. Yes, it feels like home, and we are so grateful."

On my podcast, I interview people who have moved from all over the world to Portugal. Since I live in Setubal, most guests live here," explains **Marcel Lahaije**.

"I do the podcast by myself and finding guests turns out to be quite easy. I do, however, ask my guests to

94 Portugal Living Magazine

be open and have the courage to be vulnerable … because we go deep. Most people have a reason why they moved to Portugal and 'retirement' usually doesn't make for a great story. Instead, I look for guests who are on their 'Hero's Journey,' who are looking for themselves, and who want to contribute. It is also about life's challenges: how do you deal with the obstacles on your path when you are looking for a better life in Portugal?

Marcel says he started this podcast because "it's not only a great way to meet new people but the stories they share are universal. On a deeper level, we are all the same, we experience challenges, and we have to deal with daily stuff. Through our stories, we not only connect but they also give us an opportunity to reflect on our own lives. I am good at bringing those stories to the surface and sharing them with others so we can learn, grow, connect on a deeper level. For me, it's always about a personal story. God speaks to us through stories."

Readers can find follow Marcel's interviews on Spotify, Apple podcasts, and YouTube.

So, what happened … 2018, Tel Aviv, 31st of August. The last day of summer and our first wedding. We conducted the ceremony ourselves which, from a legal point of view, was actually "just" a wedding for us.

We invited friends and family for a joyful celebration, and asked them not to give us gifts, rather spend their money on drinks. The venue was the roof terrace of our favorite bar overlooking the flea market of old Jaffa.

We couldn't imagine that a wedding could be simpler than this, or that it would be possible to get married in a more "**Nimi and Kristóf**" way. However, we just did—in front of a government official in a small town in Portugal.

We are all about celebration, but this time we "remarried" not to have another party, but because the Israeli government cancelled our partnership visas after we moved to Greece.

In our new home, we learned that we couldn't get married either, since neither of us is Greek. And Hungary was never an option since, according to our government, gay couples cannot call themselves a family.

We have been family since the day we decided to spend our lives together. However little the documents mean to us, we realized: in a world where LGBTQ people are discriminated, we need security and visibility.

"You, Kristóf and Nimrod, came with the decision to get married, forming a family and building a home, in the spirit of unity, respect and loyalty, I pronounce you husband and husband." said Annabella, the registrar who sacrificed her lunch break for their last-minute wedding.

A former nightclub bouncer and black-belt karate instructor, Portuguese artist **Joana Vasconcelos** doesn't shrink from the challenges thrown by her latest lavish creation. The 51-year-old, renowned for her big, in-your-face installations, is creating a ceramic wedding cake that's 12 meters (40 feet) high and 15 meters (50 feet) wide for exhibition in England.

"The Wedding Cake" is mostly made of Portugal's famous ceramic tiles called "azulejos." Vasconcelos is using them in pastel pink, green, blue and yellow in what is her most ambitious outdoor project yet.

And she savors the battle. "Every day you know that something will happen and something new will come up and you have to solve problems," she said in a recent interview with The Associated Press. "It's a very dynamic and alive thing."

Diana Guedes had a job working as an analyst for a company providing environmental certifications, all the while commuting over 240 km daily to work. That is until the day she decided that sort of life was no longer for her. Coming to that conclusion, she decided to open a cheese shop in Porto, representing a possibility to start a new, quieter life—in addition to fulfilling an old dream of working with something that she had always been passionate about.

But she did so not in the tourist areas of Baixa or Ribeira—crowded with visitors and mass-market shops—but instead in the neighbourhood of Praça do Marquês, a part of the city possessing a balanced mix of shops and residential buildings.

This is the story of **Queijaria da Praça**, a unique cheese shop in Porto that can also serve up a little inspiration—to do what one really enjoys in life.

Espectáculos

Compiled by Brian Elliott

Summer is here and along with the great weather a plethora of amazing concerts around Portugal are on the horizon. The major festivals also bring some mega-stars to our shores, and there are some fantastic nights ahead for you all to enjoy, no matter your music preferences.

Cláudia Pascoal launches June in Porto by bringing her new album to the Hard Club on the 2nd and, in Lisbon, **D.A.M.A.** visit Coliseu dos Recreios on the 3rd and 4th. Then legend **Bob Dylan** returns to Lisbon, this time at Campo Pequeno on the 4th and 5th. **Djavan** play there on the 7th and 9th, before moving to the Super Bock Arena in Porto on the 10th. Capitólio in Lisbon is also busy with **Dakhabakha** on the 1st and the American **Ezra Furman** on the 6th, after she plays the Hard Club in Porto on the 5th.

Unfortunately, the **Shawn Mendez** concert at Altica Arena on the 7th was cancelled last year, but the first major festival of the season, *Nos Primavera Sound*, comes to the Parque da Cidade in Porto on the second weekend in June. This is one of the best festivals in Portugal, from my point of view, due to the venue, the stars they attract, and the chilled vibe of the attendees. **Kendrick Lamar** headlines on the 7th, **Rosalía** and **Bad Religion** on the 8th, the **Pet Shop Boys** and **Jayda G** on the 9th and **New Order**, **Blur** and **Halsey** on the 10th. There are many more bands playing on the three stages over the weekend so there is something for everyone. On the 10th **Amália Hoje** play at the Multiusos Guimerães, and the opera **Rigoletto** tours throughout Portugal in June with shows at the Coliseu Porto Ageas on the 7th, Casino Estoril on the 9th and the Coliseu dos Recreios on the 10th.

Pop rock giant **Maroon 5** bring their UK and European Tour to the Passeio Marítimo de Algés on the 13th and the rock gods of **Def Leppard** and **Motley Crue** bring their joint world tour to the same venue on the 23rd. **Pérola** plays at Capitólio on the 24th and **Tayc** at Coliseu dos Recreios on the 25th. Stadium Rock returns to Lisbon with **Rammstein** playing at the Estádio da Luz on the 26th, and rock also takes over at Altice Arena with **Pantera**, **Atler Bridge**, and **Slipknot** headlining the *Evil Live Festival* on the 28th and 29th. **Andrea Bocelli** then takes over the arena on the 30th and the 1st July. Up in Porto, **Maria Bethânia** plays the Super Bock Arena on the 28th, and **Warpaint** play the Hard Club on the 30th.

The next stops on the festival wagon are the *Nova Era Beach Party*, which brings **Tiesto** and other DJs to Matosinos between the 30th June and the 1st of July, and *Sumol Summerfest*, headlined by **Wiz Khalifa** and **Popcaan**, which runs between the 30th June to the 1st July. Please note this festival has moved this year to Costa da Caparica from Ericeira.

At the same time, the *Jardim Sonoro Festival* (30 June to 2 August) brings a wide range of bands, including **Sister Sledge**, to the Jardim Keil do Amaral just outside Lisbon. Rock duo **Royal Blood** visit Campo Pequeno on the 2nd of July and **Joss Stone** plays at the Super Bock Arena in Porto on the 4th. The festival focus returns to Passeio Marítimo de Algés for *Nos Alive* between the 6th and the 8th. Headliners include the **Red Hot Chilli Peppers** and **The Black Keys** (6th), the **Arctic Monkeys**, **IDLES** and **Lizzo** (7th) and **Queens of the Stone Age**, **Sam Smith**, and **Tash Saltana** (8th).

Many other bands are playing over the two stages. Dance Music aficionados are also in for a treat with **Alok**, **Example**, **KSHMR**, **Riton**, **Oliver Heldens**, and **Joel Corey** playing on the beach at *RFM Somnii* at Figueira da Foz between the 7th and 9th, and the *Rolling Load Festival* between the 5th and the 7th July brings hip hop to Portimão with **Travis Scott** headlining. The treats do not stop that weekend with **Kim Morby** at the Hard Club in Porto on the 6th, **Lionel Richie** at the **Hipódromo** Manuel Possolo in Cascais on the 8th (part of the *Cool Jazz Festival*), **We are Scientists** at Musicbox in Lisbon on the same night, and **Melvins** tour Portugal playing the Hard Club on the 8th and Capitólio on the 9th.

Festival lovers have a dilemma the following weekend with *Super Bock, Super Rock* bringing **The Offspring**, **James Murphy**, **Franz Ferdinand**, **Charlotte De Witte**, **Nile Rogers & Chic**, **Wu-Tang Clang**, and **The 1975** to Meco between the 13th and 15th, whilst up in the north **Da Weasel**, **Os Quatro e Meia**, **J Balvin**, **Pablo Alborán**, **Black Eyed Peas**, **Xavier Rudd**, and **The Script** are at *MEO Mares Vivas*, at Vila Nova de Guia. **Omara Portuondo** tours Portugal with concerts at the Coliseu Porto Ageas on the 8th and Coliseu dos Recreios on the 14th, and **Rod Stewart** returns to Altice Arena in Lisbon on the 16th. On the same night, **The Scorpions** play the Altice Forum in Braga, and then it is back to Passeio Marítimo de Algés on the 18th for the visit of **Harry Styles**. Unfortunately, this concert sold out months ago.

Ludovico Einaudi comes back to Portugal with concerts at the Coliseu dos Recreios on the 21st and Super Bock Arena on the 22nd and 23rd. Then it is time for the *Cool Jazz Festival* to start again at the **Hipódromo Manuel Possolo** in Cascais with **Kings of Convenience** on the 19th, **Snarky Puppy** on the 20th, **Van Morrison** on the 22nd, **Ben Harper and the Innocent Criminals** on the 26th, **Tiago Bettencourt** and **Nena** on the 27th, and **Norah Jones** on the 29th. On the 22nd to the 29th *FMM Sines* bring myriad foreign bands and singers to Sines, and the festival *Jardins do Marquês* brings **Michael Bolton** (27th), **António Zambujo**, **Camané e Ricardo Ribeiro** (29th), **Liniker**, and **Bala Desejo** (30th), **Maria Bethânia** (1st July), **Pink Martini** (2nd July), and **Joss Stone** (5th July) to Oerias.

August is rather quiet for concerts but is packed with Festivals. *MEO Sudoeste* brings **David Guetta**, **Nial Horan**, **Farruko**, **Bizarrap**, **Giulia Be**, **Metro Boomin**, and **Ivandro** to Zambujeira do Mar between the 9th and the 12th. *Neopop* highlights electronic music at Viana do Castelo on the 10th to the 12th and *O Sol de Caparica* brings a host of Portuguese bands to Caparica on the 17th to the 20th.

Up at *Vodaphone Paredes de Coura,* the 30th anniversary of this festival is headlined by **Jesse Ware**, **Yo La Tengo**, **the Sleaford Mods**, and **Lorde** between August 16th and 19th. There is also the *Festival do Crato* on the 22nd to 26th and *EDP Villar de Mouros* on the 24th to 27th; however, the lineups of these festivals at the time of writing have not been announced. Finally, *MEO Kalorama* returns at the end of the month (31 August to 2 September) with **Arcade Fire**, **Aphex Twin**, **Florence and the Machine**, **Belle & Sebastian**, **Young Fathers**, the **Yeah Yeah Yeahs**, **Foals**, **Metronomy**, and **Dino d'Santiago** and many others playing on the Parque de Bela Vista in Lisbon. Many local festivals also bring local, national, and sometimes even international bands to a stage near you. There are too many to mention here, so check out your local listings and go and catch some live music this summer.

These listings are correct at the time of writing and readers are advised to check individual band and festival websites nearer the time for more details.

CAPTION CONTEST

Portugal Living Magazine asked members of seven groups—including Instagram and our own Facebook page followers—to come up with an appropriate caption for this image. It wasn't easy choosing the best among the 67 proposed. The winner, who receives our €25 prize, is **Lynda Seal**. Her caption?

"I'll buy you a beer when we get there, boys!"

Runners-up include:

"I've got your head in the bag, madam. We will reattach it when we get to the corner."
Vicky Turner

"Come on, boys … do try to keep up."
Faith Harrison

"Obviously, we'll do our best to try and find it. But can you remember roughly when and where you last saw your head, madam?"
Ged Rodger

"The culprit put up a good chase, but the police finally apprehended her."
Paul Rogers

"With a little help from my friends."
Karen Michelle Yarbrough

"Can you imagine the headlines tomorrow?"
Judes Ward

"Can you help me find my contact lenses, please?"
Jackie Mulrenan

"When you lose your head drinking, you end up being escorted home by police."
João Alexander Louis

"Okay, my dear. Let's not get ahead of ourselves."
Craig Weincek

"No job too big or small for our protectors in blue!"
Amanda Marques

97 *Portugal Living Magazine*

Classifieds

Trips, Tours & Transport

International Shipping made easy & affordable. Free quotes. No hidden fees. Price guaranteed. The smarter way to move overseas!
www.upakweship.com

For Sale

Large selection of spices, spice mixes, dried herbs, and chillies available for immediate dispatch across Portugal.
The Chilli Experience

American Groceries offers the foods, garnishes, and side dishes you crave! Shop online with prompt delivery, click & collect options, or by appointment.

Properties for Sale

Find your dream property in the Azores Islands: luxury residential, apartments, farms, country houses with land, commercial.
Azores Properties

Have you been looking to have your own business, villa, B&B, and an event room—all in the same place? This outstanding property on 12,400 sqm of land is situated 8 kms away from Tomar and less than 1,5 kms from Castelo do Bode lake. Visit it on Chavetejo.
Ref 700/23.

Also from Chavetejo: Stylishly renovated, two bedroom, off grid, stone house with fantastic views of the countryside. Near Alvaiázere.
Ref: 541/22.

Old country property with lots of potential could easily be lived in while any work is undertaken. Three bedrooms all quite good sizes. Perfectly working kitchen with an open fireplace which could be kept as a lovely feature. Ruins on the grounds could be made into an independent property. Just €80,000! Listed by Chavetejo.
Ref: 562/18.

Modern townhouse with amazing views, for sale by Chavetejo only 5 minutes walking distance from town centre of Tomar! This amazing property offers high quality finishes and materials and is equiped with air conditioning, double glazing, electric shutter, s and solar panel. Magnificent views of the Convent of Christ, Templar Castle, and the beautiful city of Tomar.
Ref: 534/22.

Looking to buy property in Portugal's interior? Picoto Imobiliária is your international relocation specialist for central Portugal.

Follow my journey as a real estate broker in Arizona to researching, traveling, buying, and selling land in Portugal. I'm your boots on the ground here!

Need help finding a lawyer, mortgage broker, surveyor, or property? Della Meyers is your buyer's agent in the Sesimbra, Azeitão, and Setúbal areas.

From Coimbra to Guarda--and everything in between!--Central Portugal's leading property agent is Tiago Freitas.

Properties for Rent

For annual and winter lets, D7 Visa-compliant rentals, and rent-before-buying accommodations, you can trust. Visit us online:
Algarve Long Lets.

Rental Property Management by Tiago Freitas includes everything—from inspections to collections, maintenance and repairs, dealing with Finanças, representing you competently and professionally.

Home Services

Onergy—Your complete source for the best brands of energy-efficient HVAC and home appliances at down-to-earth prices. Sales. Repairs. Installation.

Expert property inspections for buyers and venders. 35 years' experience. Personal, professional service using the latest equipment and technologies.
www.tjpropertyinspections.com

GP Design Atelier (Lisbon) is your fashionable home for interior design, creating unique furniture, and preparing any/everything with fabrics that reflect your unique personality.

Certified electrician/expert plumber comforting your life with climate control, thermal, solar & photovoltaic energy.
franciscojosilva@gmail.com

All-around construction, roofing, clearing work, plumbing, block work, plastering, rendering, transport of items. Lots of refs, reliable. Castelo Branco area.
Alaninleeds@alive.com

Searching for, buying, or restoring older properties? Reabilitejo provides surveys & inspections, technical assessments, planning advice, project scoping, and additional services.

Portuguese Language Services

Portuguese Language Lessons—Established 11 years (BF) Online: 1:1/ Group Classes, Exam Preparation Courses. Emma: +351-969-249-273/+044-739-1157-013. info@portugueselanguagelessons.net

Personal Services

English-speaking funeral director available 24/7. Vast experience with foreign clients. Located in Central Portugal.
+351-913-287-073.
Whatsapp available.
Fernandomendes1987@gmail.com

Expat Coach Deborah Dahab: "Beyond the practical side of moving, dealing with the cultural transition process can help you create your best life abroad."

Hospitality

Enjoy the peace and nature of the Alto Alentejo at Assumar Country House. Take walks along quiet roads. Explore the area by bicycle. Enjoy our spacious swimming pool. Delight in our garden seat with a book and a glass of wine.

Insurance

For any type of insurance you need, please consult us for the most suitable selection. At Medal, you will always find someone who will provide the attention you deserve and solve any insurance problem.
www.medal.pt

Online Notary & Apostille Services

Remote Online Virtual Notary for US Documents. Banking. Insurance. Brokerage. Real Estate Closings. Apostilles. Whatsapp 904-333-7311.
Selecia Young-Jones.

Relocation Assistance

Planning to relocate to Portugal? Think no more. Viv Europe will assist with your visa process, business, real estate, and more.
https://viveurope.com

Relocating to the centre of Portugal? Contact Picoto Real Estate & Relocation Consultants in Vila de Rei to advise you on your personal preferences.
www.picotovdr.com or email geral@picotovdr.com

Located in the heart of the Silver Coast, Portugal the Place is a full-service destination company providing relocation and scouting services across all of Portugal.

Membership Groups

Afpop is the largest association for foreign residents in Portugal. Since 1987, we have specialised in providing comprehensive services and support to members.

Over 12,000 members strong, ExpatsPortugal is a friendly, vibrant community to meet online, ask questions, share experiences, and learn more about life in Portugal.

Five minutes of your time is all it takes to complete a survey aimed at foreign nationals living in Portugal or thinking about moving or retiring here:

https://forms.gle/d4KZXkFgK7az7QT67

Business & Professional Directory

Onergy - Outlet Electrodomésticos
Solar Térmico, Fotovoltaico, Eólica
Projectos, Instalação
Assistência Técnica Multimarcas

Brands: Vulcano, Sunset, Hummer, AEG, Electrolux, Zanussi

Eng.º João Mendes
Gerente
Tlm. 919 989 188

Dep. Técnico: Tlm. 932 035 089

Av. General Humberto Delgado, N.º 1
6000-081 CASTELO BRANCO

Tel. 272 346 288
E-mail: jmendes@onergy.pt
www.onergy.pt

Passion 4 Portugal Properties
www.p4portugalproperties.com
E-mail: maria@p4portugalproperties.com

Gerente
Maria Moore 918 691 938

Mediação Imobiliária AMI 14121
Rua Luciano Migueis, Lote 3, nº 18 - R/ch - MARINHA GRANDE

VETBEIRÃO
Clínica Veterinária de Castelo Branco

HORÁRIO:
2ª a 6ª Feira
10h00 – 13h00
15h00 – 19h30

Sábados
10h00 – 13h00
15h00 – 17h00

272 325 798
Urgências 24h

Urbanização Quinta Dr. Beirão, Lote 16-14B, 6000-140 Castelo Branco

Tiago Freitas - RE/MAX
+351 927 068 077
TRFREITAS@REMAX.PT

540.000€ - in Paranhos da Beira (Central Portugal) ID: 124221073-41
400sqm historic portuguese mansion with guest house, on a 4800 sqm land with own water well and fully gatted property.

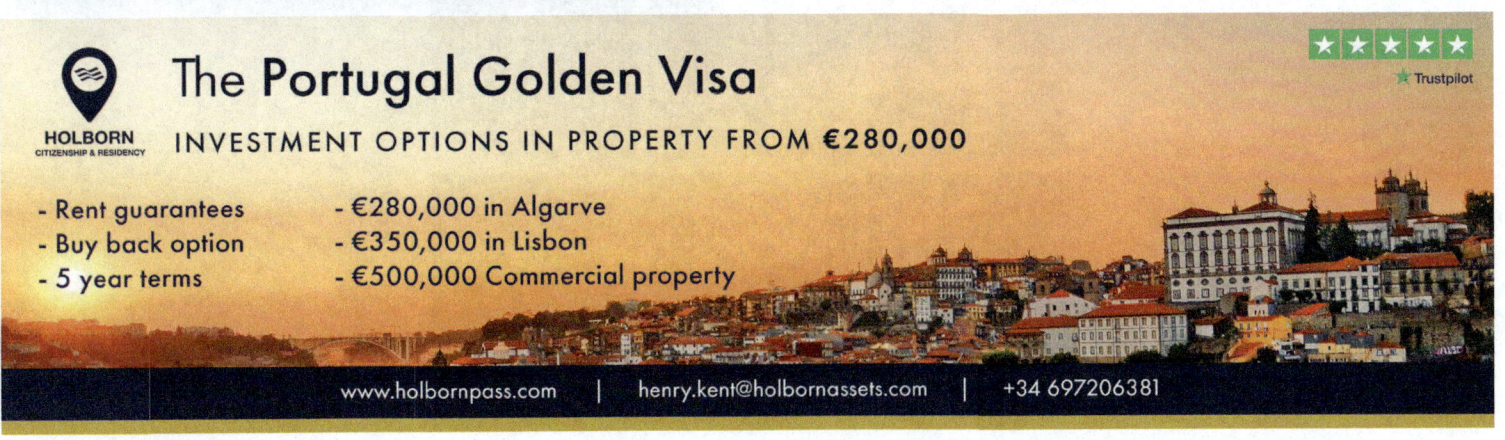

L'Amazzona Restaurante Pizzaria
TELEMÓVEL 961053926
Castelo Branco
TELEFONE 272345524

Sarah Sibert
Web Development

For individuals, businesses and charities.

www.sarahsibert.net

The Portugal Golden Visa — HOLBORN Citizenship & Residency
INVESTMENT OPTIONS IN PROPERTY FROM €280,000

- Rent guarantees
- Buy back option
- 5 year terms
- €280,000 in Algarve
- €350,000 in Lisbon
- €500,000 Commercial property

★★★★★ Trustpilot

www.holbornpass.com | henry.kent@holbornassets.com | +34 697206381

Portugal Living Magazine

Portugal Living Magazine to Cease PDF-Format Production

With this third anniversary (Summer 2023) issue, Portugal Living Magazine, the "thoughtful magazine for people everywhere with Portugal on their minds," will discontinue some of its operations.

A "victim of its own success," according to publisher and creative director Bruce H. Joffe, the quarterly English language magazine has reached an online distribution base of nearly 10,000 subscribers who signed up for its PDF edition, while hundreds more purchase the paperback version available from Amazon. Advertising comprises more than 30% of its 100+ pages, and "lack of money" wasn't a motivation to stop production, according to its publisher.

"I'm exhausted," he says. The author of seven books, Joffe says he's working on an eighth—*Spanish Towns, Portuguese Villages: Expats and Immigrants.*

He will also continue publishing Portugal Living Magazine daily on Facebook.

Featuring the work of more than two dozen talented writers, photographers, and illustrators, Portugal Living Magazine is the only major English language periodical not based in or focused on the Algarve. "Full spectrum" and "cutting edge" is how the magazine defines itself, reaching people planning to visit or relocate in Portugal, newcomers seeking an orientation to the country, and long-time residents eager to learn more about the country, its people and places, culture, and heritage.

In November 2022, Portugal Living Magazine received Marcom's Gold Award in the Magazine category, recognizing outstanding creative achievement by marketing and communication professionals. The magazine also received an Honorable Mention as an "E-Magazine" in Content and Digital Marketing in the 2023 AVA Digital Awards sponsored by the Association of Marketing and Communication Professionals (AMCP), the industry's preeminent third-party evaluator of creative work.

Portugal Living Magazine's international audience engages readers around the world: 50% are in Portugal, 33% in the USA, 9% in the UK, 3% in Canada, and the balance in more than 30 other countries.

"It is with the greatest sense of *saudade* that I say I gave it my best shot," Joffe laughs. "This issue is my swan song; Portugal Living Magazine, a living legacy."

Photo Finish

Alentejo road: considered by many to be the most beautiful in Portugal. Photo – Nuno Tendais Fotógrafo/iStock.com

Your team in Portugal

American owned Portuguese Inspired

We are passionatelly dedicated to helping you move to Portugal. We are Americans and Portuguese working together to help you navigate the process of relocating to Portugal.

Portugal The Place
A DESTINATION MANAGEMENT COMPANY
www.portugaltheplace.com

Services Include

- In depth location scouting
- Long-term rental scouting
- Home purchase scouting
- Virtual or hosted

+351 961 315 405
inquires@portugaltheplace.com

Book your call today www.portugaltheplace.com

Printed in Great Britain
by Amazon